Essential
Euro Disney®
Resort

by

LINDSAY HUNT

Lindsay Hunt turned to travel journalism after a career
in publishing and a year sampling tapas in Spain. She
has researched many destinations for *Holiday Which?*
magazine, and is co-author of several hotel guides and
a book on Spain.

GW00514778

AA

Produced by AA Publishing

Written by Lindsay Hunt
Series Adviser: Ingrid Morgan
Copy editors: Ron Hawkins and
Edwina Johnson

Edited, designed and produced
by AA Publishing. Maps ©
The Automobile Association
1993

Distributed in the United
Kingdom by AA Publishing,
Fanum House, Basingstoke,
Hampshire, RG21 2EA.

The contents of this publication
are believed correct at the time
of printing. Nevertheless, the
publishers cannot accept
responsibility for errors or
omissions, or for changes in
details given. Assessments of
attractions, hotels, restaurants
and so forth are based upon the
author's own experience and,
therefore, descriptions given in
this guide necessarily contain
an element of subjective
opinion which may not reflect
the publisher's opinion or
dictate a reader's own
experience on another
occasion.
**We have tried to ensure
accuracy in this guide, but
things do change and we
would be grateful if readers
would advise us of any
inaccuracies they may
encounter.**

A CIP catalogue record for this
book is available from the
British Library.

ISBN 0 7495 0520 6

Published by The Automobile
Association.

This book was produced using
QuarkXPress™, Aldus
Freehand™ and Microsoft
Word™ on Apple Macintosh™
computers.

Colour separation by BTB
Colour Reproduction Ltd,
Whitchurch, Hampshire

Printed by Printers Trento
S.R.L., Italy

*Front cover picture: Le Château
de la Belle au Bois Dormant
(Sleeping Beauty's Castle)*

Contents

All prices quoted in this book were current at the time of going to press. However, as they are intended to serve as guidelines only, readers are strongly advised to check details with Euro Disney at the time of their visit. (The letter 'F' indicates prices in French francs.)

This book employs a simple rating system to help choose which places to visit:

  'top ten'

◆◆◆ do not miss
◆◆ see if you can
◆ worth seeing if you have time

Introduction and Background

INTRODUCTION

The idea of a Disney theme park in Europe goes back well over a decade, though it was not until 1984 that The Walt Disney Company began to explore the possibilities seriously. The options were wide open. Would English-speaking Britain, whose citizens so eagerly patronise American theme parks, naturally play host to Mickey Mouse? Or should the new park be blessed with that cocktail of sunshine and oranges so successful in California and Florida – by being located in southern Spain, perhaps? Why not target the

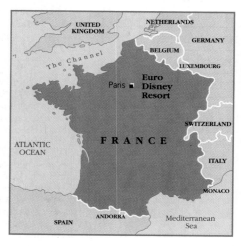

Parades now take place on what were once fields

wealthy Germans? No doubt they could run the show as efficiently as Walt would have wished. Feasibility studies spawned; Team Disney anguished, and then began some hard bargaining. Eventually, the keys to the kingdom fell into French hands. The promised land was a stretch of unprepossessing sugar-beet fields about 20 miles (32km) east of Paris. Not immediately enticing, but the Marne-la-Vallée area had a number of advantages. For one thing, it was available. And there are not that many suitably-sized tracts of affordable land available in Western Europe these days. Secondly, it lay slap in the middle of a cat's cradle of important communication networks linking the richest and most densely populated countries of Europe. And thirdly, it was on the eastern outskirts of the greater Paris area. It was, admittedly, a bit damper and chillier than one might have hoped, but

Mickey abounds

you can't have everything, even in a dream factory.

The Walt Disney Company signed a 30-year contract to develop the site with the French authorities in 1987. The French government purchased some 4,800 acres (1,940ha) of land, a total area about one-fifth the size of Paris, agreeing to release it to Disney as it was needed. Meanwhile, residents and farmers, now tenants instead of landlords, carried on their lives as normally as they could in a region destined for rapid and irrevocable change. Earth-moving and construction equipment arrived to shift millions of tons of topsoil into new configurations of lakes, railway tracks, road systems and protective circular ramparts, like some Iron Age hill-fort. The statistics were awesome, and the speed at which the project took shape was astonishing. Within four years Phase I of the development had been completed, covering 1,483 acres (600ha) of land. The region was transformed, with 360,000 trees and shrubs, several artificial expanses of water, and almost 20 miles (32km) of roads. Six extraordinary hotels emerged from the fields, but more curious structures could be glimpsed behind the stockade surrounding the new theme park – a storybook castle, a piece of recreated Arizona, and a skull-like cave.

Meanwhile, around the edges of the complex, speculation buzzed, both of the cerebral and mercenary kinds. Rumours of Disney's sinister transatlantic masterplan to undermine French Culture As We Know It Today were fuelled, and many a pundit had a scornful crack at Mickey Mouse. Not everyone liked the idea of a theme park on their doorstep. And, of course, some of the locals had to play the role of dispossessed serfs carefully, to maximise any potential return on their lost land. A crocodile tear or two would not be inappropriate in the circumstances. Many of the locals invested their new-found wealth by building a few extra bedrooms in their backyards, ready to cater for the anticipated rush of visitors. Other entrepreneurs constructed motels and petrol stations in many of the surrounding villages. These extraneous

Look who's here

developments, simply cashing in on the Disney
bandwagon, have done most to disrupt the
area. Sadly, they are an inevitable
consequence of such a huge investment,
readily predictable from all the experiences of
American theme parks.

Other unintentional effects of Disney's impact
on this part of France are less tangible, but
genuinely worrying. A glance at any local
tourist literature produces the disconcerting
sensation that the whole of the Seine-et-Marne
region is turning into a sort of giant theme park.
Many local authorities, spurred to commercial
enterprise by Disney's example, are now
promoting their tourist portfolios strongly as
rival (or rather, supplementary) attractions.
Every little sight and mildly pretty village is
now paraded before the eyes of Disney
patrons like some contestant in a game show.
Summer pageants, medieval banquets and
candlelit tours abound. With all this going on,
there is a strong possibility that some visitors at
least, dazed by the razzmatazz, will come to
regard the great châteaux of the Ile-de-France
as mere clones of Sleeping Beauty's Castle.
For those who recognise the difference,
however, the historic and cultural riches of the
surroundings (including Paris, of course) must
be regarded as one of Euro Disney Resort's
most appealing features. In the US, at Orlando
and Anaheim, there are certainly dozens of
things to do, but they are an oddly
monochromatic mix of rival theme parks and
contrived recreation. In France the texture of
the holiday tapestry is infinitely more
interesting and complex.

The positive influence of the Disney theme
park on the area's economy is hard to deny.
The prospect of 12,000 new jobs, and spin-offs
for hoteliers and other local businesses, must
be most welcome. The infrastructure of the
area (road and rail connections, hotel
accommodation, and so on) has been boosted
out of all recognition. What is now completed is
merely Phase I of the Euro Disney Resort
project. A whole new theme park is scheduled
for development by 1996, modelled on the
Disney–MGM Studios (a film and TV
production centre and movie theme park) in

Florida. After that, until the contract expires in
the year 2017, *'On verra'*.

The scale and scope of Euro Disney Resort is
by any standards a modern miracle, second in
Europe only to the Channel Tunnel in terms of
cost and engineering resources. The Sun King
himself, Louis XIV, would have appreciated
such an ambitious project. Will it succeed? Will
11 million souls troop through those turnstiles
each year? There will be plenty of
Schadenfreude in the air if the Resort is not an
immediate financial success – any organisation
as powerful as The Walt Disney Company is
bound to arouse a certain amount of jealousy
and malice.

Some agonise, justifiably enough, over the
unFrenchness of it all. There are nods and
winks at European fairy stories and children's
classics, but basically Euro Disney Resort is a
heartily transatlantic product, as American as a

prime rib steak. French culture, however, is
nothing if not robust. The things many people
love about France and the French way of life
will survive the arrival of Mickey Mouse
perfectly well. In any case, before we complain
too loudly about the invasion of an alien
culture, maybe there are some things about
the land of Mickey Mouse that we Europeans
should take note of: what, after all, is wrong
with clean loos, courteous staff, efficient
transport systems and litter-free grounds? Why
not put a bit of the Disney professionalism into
our lifestyles here? For the Resort to be a
success, all Disney needs is for enough people
to turn up and enjoy themselves, and then tell
their friends. And enjoying yourself at Euro
Disney Resort is really rather easy. Where else
can grown-up people ride on an elephant
roundabout, or wear mouse ears, without
feeling like complete chumps?

Euro Disneyland Park, from the air

BACKGROUND

Walt Disney

*Walt Disney,
(1901-66)*

Few film producers have captured the imagination, influenced so many people, and aroused such loyalty, loathing and passionate interest as Walt Disney. More than 25 years after his death, debate still rages over the influence of his work – even more over the colossal empire he created to perpetuate it. Through this he has achieved a strangely alarming immortality. So, too, has his single most memorable creation: Mickey Mouse, now over 60 years old.

Walter Elias Disney was born in Chicago, Illinois, in 1901, the fourth of five children in a family of slender means. His father was a struggling building contractor whose varied enterprises consistently failed. When they did, the family doggedly moved on, first to Marceline, then to Kansas City, Missouri. Walt's unsettled upbringing gave him only a rudimentary education, and he spent his spare time living on his wits, delivering newspapers door-to-door and hawking sodas on trains. During a brief stint of ambulance-driving in France at the end of World War I (he was too young to join up), he first exercised his artistic talents commercially, painting camouflage helmets and adding fake bullet holes. After the war Walt returned to Kansas City and found a job drawing for an advertising agency. There he met a talented Dutch artist, Ub Iwerks, and together they set up a company, Laugh-o-Gram Films. It soon went to the wall but, like all true romantics of his day, Walt was hopelessly hooked on the glamour of celluloid. With a small fistful of dollars, he set off to try his luck in Hollywood, followed by Ub. From then on Walt had little contact with his parents. But he always kept up with his elder brother Roy, with whom he later set up in business to produce short cartoons. In 1925 Walt married Lillian Bounds, who lived with his erratic genius for over 40 years.

Fantasyland's awe-inspiring castle

After many false starts and financial failures (one of which involved the loss of his prize cartoon character, Oswald the Lucky Rabbit, to an unprincipled distributor), Walt's big break came in 1928, using a new character called Mickey Mouse. The film was *Steamboat Willie,* the first animated film to use synchronised sound. Mickey's squeaks and sighs were Walt Disney's own. Roy Disney attempted to temper Walt's wilder impulses with sensible financial caution, but Walt, always cavalier about the money side, was an incorrigible enthusiast, an ideas man, a risk-taker. And his instincts were sound. He could spot a good story at a thousand paces (and shamelessly borrow it, if necessary) and then would edit it brilliantly for his own medium. Above all else, he was a maniacal perfectionist. Every last detail had to be right. All his life he worked obsessively hard, even coming dangerously close to a nervous breakdown in 1931.

Slowly the Disney studios began to prosper with full-length animations like *Snow White and the Seven Dwarfs, Pinocchio* and *Fantasia.* After World War II the Disney brothers seized the opportunities offered by the new era of television. Their *Disneyland* programme (set up, in part, to fund the first theme park) was a great success. From animated films, Disney moved on to using live actors in comedies, wildlife pictures and adventure stories like *Treasure Island.* The core of the business was always safe, clean, family entertainment for the post-war era. The films sold like hot cakes.

Today's Disney theme parks know no bounds

The Disney Movies

1923 '*Alice Comedies*' (with Ub Iwerks): 56 films mixing animation and live action.

1928 **Steamboat Willie**: first appearance of Mickey and Minnie Mouse, and the first animated film using synchronised sound. Only squeaks, sighs and whistles were recorded.

1929 '*Silly Symphonies*': 75 short animations in which plants and creatures come to life. The famous Skeleton Dance was the first of this series.

1930 **The Chain Gang**: first appearance of Pluto.

1932 **Flowers and Trees**: wins Disney's first Academy Award, and the first cartoon made in *full* colour. Mickey's Revue appears – also the first appearance of Goofy.

1933 **Three Little Pigs**: another Academy Award.

1934 **The Wise Little Hen**: Donald Duck first appears.

1935 **Music Land**.

1937 **Snow White and the Seven Dwarfs**: the first full-length feature animation. Despite Roy Disney's gloomy predictions and the massive costs, a huge success.

1940 **Pinocchio** and **Fantasia** appear, denting the studio's budgets, but not its spirit.

1941 **Dumbo** wins an Academy Award for Best Original Score.

1942 **Bambi** is premiered.

1943 **Der Führer's Face**: Donald Duck does his bit for the war effort, and the film wins an Academy Award. Saludos Amigos appears.

1948 **Seal Island**: a nature film.

1950 **Treasure Island** and **Cinderella** appear, the first a departure from Disney norms, using live actors.

1951 **Alice in Wonderland**.

1953 **Peter Pan, The Living Desert** and **The Alaskan Eskimo**.

1954 **20,000 Leagues Under the Sea**: Academy Award for special effects.

1955 **Davy Crockett – King of the Wild Frontier** and **Lady and the Tramp**.

1959 **Sleeping Beauty**.

1960 **Swiss Family Robinson**.

1961 **One Hundred and One Dalmatians**.

1963 **The Sword in the Stone**.

1964 *Mary Poppins*: six Academy Awards, including a Best Actress award for Julie Andrews.
1967 *The Jungle Book*.
1970 *The Aristocats*.
1973 *Robin Hood*.
1977 *The Many Adventures of Winnie the Pooh*.
1988 *Who Framed Roger Rabbit*: four Academy Awards, signalling Disney's return to success after many uncertain years following Walt's death.
1990 *The Little Mermaid*: two Academy Awards for musical content.
1991 *Beauty and the Beast* coincides with the 20th anniversary of Walt Disney World. Two Academy Awards, and nomination as Best Picture.

Magic Kingdoms

Walt first dreamt of theme parks in the 1930s, imagining how he could improve on the dreary ones he took his daughters to see, but it was only after the war that his obsession developed to fever pitch. At that time amusement parks were bracketed with funfairs and circuses as tawdry and disreputable places. Walt found it very difficult to convey his vision of a place of fun and fantasy in an orderly, civilised setting. He wanted to create a place where both adults and children could enjoy themselves together and come away feeling better, but his ideas went far beyond fairground thrill rides. He wanted themes that reflected his Utopian faith in technological progress and the future, a haven where evil could never triumph, in which the archetypal American virtues of pluck and innocence could flourish.
In 1955 Disneyland Park (also known as 'the Magic Kingdom'), the world's first theme park, opened at Anaheim, in Orange County, California. Roy refused to let Walt have the money to build it; he had to cash in his life insurance. But the enterprise succeeded, and the world flocked to see it. Walt began to dream of other theme parks, his ambitions growing like beanstalks for a brave new world – a model of planning and innovative lifestyles.

Disney merchandise

A second site was chosen: the ill-drained acres of central Florida, another 'Orange County'. Quietly the land was purchased on Disney's behalf at knock-down prices through various agencies. The bulldozers moved in to hack down the palmetto scrub and build drainage canals. Sadly, Walt Disney never lived to see his Floridian dream realised. In 1966 his permanent smoker's cough developed a more sinister note, and by December, just a week after his 65th birthday, he was dead. It was left

Autopia's superhighway of the future

Disney characters are central to all the Park's attractions

to his heirs to construct Walt Disney World Resort from the blueprint. This second theme park complex opened in Orlando in 1971, much larger and more ambitious than anything in California. Twelve years later, in 1983, another Disneyland Park appeared in Tokyo. Soon afterwards, a talented new chief executive recruited from Paramount, Michael Eisner, was setting a firm course for the floundering Disney empire, which for several years after its founder's death had seemed to lose its way. Throughout the 1980s the theme parks boomed, and revenues from television and merchandising soared. By the middle of the decade plans for a European park were firmly on the drawing board.

The Disney Ethos
Disney values are decent and clean-living. In his many films, and in the theme parks, Walt Disney's touching optimism and trust in the goodness of humanity reign supreme (odd in a man who, by all accounts, trusted no one in business). Disney theme parks are worlds of happy endings and moral certainties. They are simplistic stuff by the cynical standards of the

Norman Blood?
By a happy and much-publicised coincidence, Walt Disney's ancestry was French. The name 'Disney' is alleged to come from the Normandy coastal village of Isigny-sur-Mer. After the Norman Conquest of England in 1066, Hughes d'Isigny and his son Robert settled there. Gradually the name became abbreviated and Anglicised. One branch of the family is still in Lincolnshire, having kept the more Gallic spelling D'Isney. But Walt's forebears emigrated to Ireland in the 17th century, and from there Arundel Elias Disney and his brother Robert set sail for North America in 1834. Walt's father was actually born in Canada; his mother came from Ohio. It is a tenuous link, but there is at least some justification for the company's claim that France is the natural home of any European version of Disneyland Park.

late-20th century – but they are still popular and, on the surface, seem harmless enough, even charmingly naïve. In Michael Eisner, Disney's current chieftain, the company seems to have found Walt's true successor, someone with the same unerring instinct for mass-market taste. Intellectuals have levelled criticism at the anodyne, sanitised qualities of the Disney message, typically declaring it a 'sickening blend of cheap formulas packaged to sell', and a symptom of a kind of infantilism at the heart of the American psyche.

Imagineers
Any operation on the scale of a Disney theme park requires colossal planning and co-operative effort, but just how much goes on behind the scenes may surprise you. A whole workforce of Disney employees called 'Imagineers' devotes its time and energy to inventing and realising the attractions. These artists and technicians are the ones who make illusion reality, working with models and micro-cameras, experimenting with innumerable materials, designs and ideas, studying every last detail for authenticity. It is a

serious business: careers have been made and broken over the height of some of the buildings. The complexity of all this is fascinating, though most of the illusions are hidden or barely perceived by the vast majority of visitors. When you enter the theme park, notice how far away the castle seems as you look down Main Street. Why do some of the other buildings seem so accessible? It is all done with clever angles and techniques called 'forced perspective'. Upper storeys are often rather smaller than their proper size, with every architectural detail carefully scaled down. These illusions are just 3-D versions of the kinds of things Disney constantly practised in his films. What the eye sees is not necessarily what is really there, as any animation specialist knows.

Audio–Animatronics®
This Disney-patented system of animating figures (animals, plants, birds and robots, as well as humans) has now reached levels of great technical sophistication, and some amazingly lifelike effects can be created. Among striking examples of this new technology are the rowdy pirates in Adventureland, and the robots of Discoveryland. Best of all, without a doubt, is the wonderful dragon that lurks beneath the castle.

Cast Members
Anywhere else, these people would be called theme park staff. But here they are the cast – everyone from that fellow patiently sweeping up spilt popcorn to Sleeping Beauty herself. The whole park is a theatrical performance. How do they rehearse for that relentless PR exercise, constantly smiling and helpful? They go to university! The Disney University, where appropriate cheerful responses are drilled into prospective members, and deviant tendencies like tattoos, red nail polish and facial hair are rigorously drilled out. However, some concessions have been made to French fashion: red lipstick may be worn, tastefully. And who are you? Never mere 'customers' – you are the *guests* at this show.

THEME PARK TIPS

It is well worth spending some time familiarising yourself with the layout of Euro Disney Resort and Euro Disneyland Park, particularly if you only have one or two days to see everything. Those hours spent through the turnstiles will be expensive if you waste time, but if you use them well you will not be disappointed.

Euro Disney Resort

The total land area set aside for the Euro Disney Resort is 4,800 acres (1,940ha). So far less than a third of that land has been developed. Phase 1, opened in 1992, covers only about 1,483 acres (600ha). It includes Euro Disneyland Park, six hotels, a campground, a golf course and the Festival Disney entertainment centre. The exit roads from surrounding routes lead smoothly along newly constructed dual carriageways to all parts of the Resort, with all hotels and the main car park clearly signed. If you are heading for the campground you will take exit 13 from the A4. If you need petrol, you will find it by **Hotel Santa Fe**. From the large visitors' car park, covered moving walkways speed up the journey to the ticket offices and entrance gates of the Park, which are beside the unmissable **Disneyland Hotel**, a huge pink building with turrets and gables. The **Animal Care Center** is by the walkways. All pets must be left here. At the end of the moving walkways there is a picnic area. There is also a special car park

Souvenirs are all part of the fun

reserved for disabled visitors nearer the entrance to the Park. If you arrive by train, you will emerge at the Marne-la-Vallée-Chessy RER station in Station Plaza, very close to the Park entrance. From 1994, the TGV express link will terminate at the same point, joining all European rail networks. Several expanses of artificially created water form scenic vistas within the Resort area. **Lake Buena Vista** is surrounded by three hotels: **Hotel New York**, **Sequoia Lodge** and the **Newport Bay Club**. Two more hotels (**Hotel Santa Fe** and **Hotel Cheyenne**) straddle the **Rio Grande**, a canal northeast of the lake. Traffic-free promenades are on either side of the water, making the route between the theme park and the hotels a pleasant, easy walk. You can always take a free bus if you prefer.

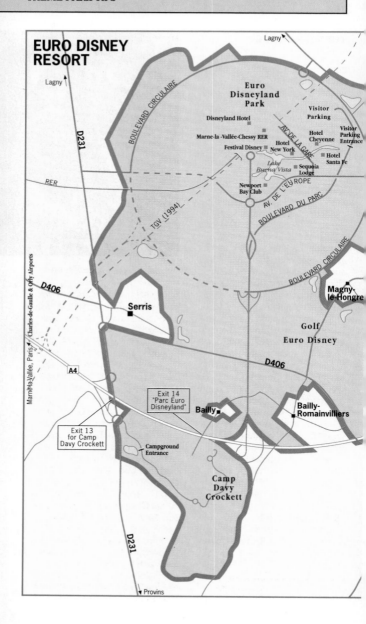

Festival Disney

Near the bus station, just three or four minutes' walk from the theme-park entrance gates, is an eye-catching complex of angular metallic towers linked by a cat's cradle of wires. During the day the sun glitters on the shiny aluminium and mosaic panels; at night the area is a maze of starry lights. This bold modern structure was designed by the Californian architect Frank Gehry, and is Euro Disney Resort's principal entertainment centre apart from the theme park. It aims to keep visitors happy after Euro Disneyland Park's gates have closed. It consists of shops, restaurants, bars, and various nightspots including a night-club and the popular **Buffalo Bill's Wild West Show**. Here there are also practical facilities, such as a children's play area and a baby-sitting centre, a post office, and a tourist information bureau for the Seine-et-Marne and Ile-de-France regions. The Festival Disney complex is open every day and there is no entrance charge.

Euro Disneyland Park

Euro Disneyland Park is divided rather like a pie chart into five separate thematic areas, or 'lands'. When you first pass through the turnstiles you will find yourself in **Station Plaza**, where a couple of shops sell things you may need in the Park (sunhats, sun cream, and so on). Walk beneath the railway station viaduct where coin-operated storage lockers are located. (Wheelchairs and

EURO DISNEYLAND PARK

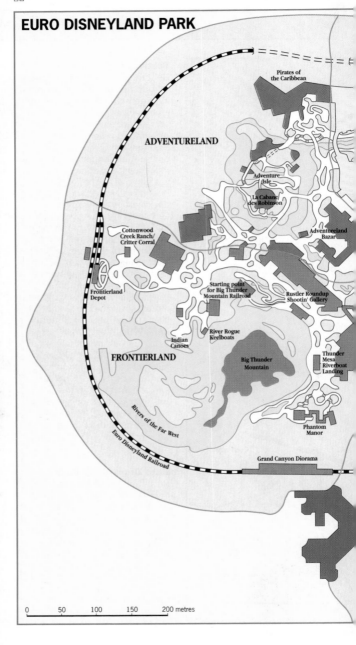

Pirates of
the Caribbean

ADVENTURELAND

Adventure
Isle

La Cabane
des Robinson

Adventureland
Bazar

Cottonwood
Creek Ranch/
Critter Corral

Frontierland
Depot

Starting point
for Big Thunder
Mountain Railroad

Rustler Roundup
Shootin' Gallery

River Rogue
Keelboats

Indian
Canoes

Thunder
Mesa
Riverboat
Landing

FRONTIERLAND

Big Thunder
Mountain

Rivers of the Far West

Phantom
Manor

Euro Disneyland Railroad

Grand Canyon Diorama

0	50	100	150	200 metres

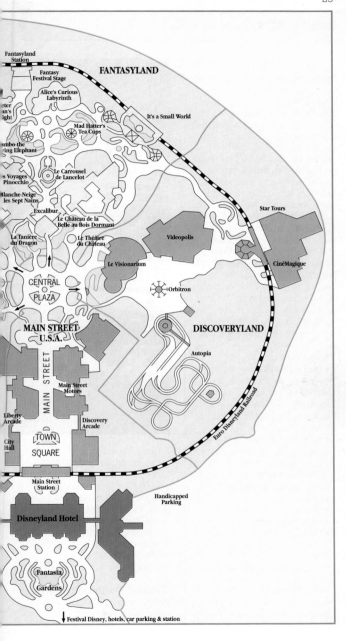

Fantasyland
Station

FANTASYLAND

Fantasy
Festival Stage

Alice's Curious
Labyrinth

...ter
...an's
...ight

Mad Hatter's
Tea Cups

It's a Small World

...mbo the
...ing Elephant

...s Voyages
...Pinocchio

Le Carrousel
de Lancelot

...lanche-Neige
...les Sept Nains

Star Tours

Excalibur

Le Château de la
Belle au Bois Dormant

Videopolis

CinéMagique

La Tanière
du Dragon

Le Théâtre
du Château

Le Visionarium

Orbitron

**CENTRAL
PLAZA**

**MAIN STREET
U.S.A.**

DISCOVERYLAND

Autopia

Main Street
Motors

...iberty
Arcade

Discovery
Arcade

Euro Disneyland Railroad

City
Hall

**TOWN
SQUARE**

Main Street
Station

Handicapped
Parking

Disneyland Hotel

**Fantasia
Gardens**

↓ Festival Disney, hotels, car parking & station

THEME PARK TIPS

pushchairs can be hired in **Town Square Terrace**, adjacent to the station.) Then go into **Town Square**, with City Hall, the Park's main information centre, to your left. **Main Street, U.S.A.** stretches ahead of you, and beyond it lies the Park's central landmark, **Le Château de la Belle au Bois Dormant** (Sleeping Beauty's Castle). You can walk along Main Street in a few minutes, or take one of the nostalgic vehicles up to **Central Plaza**. Or you can climb the steps to **Main Street Station** and catch one of the steam trains on the **Euro Disneyland Railroad**, which runs round the perimeter of the Park, stopping at two other places on the way. If it is raining, keep under cover by walking down one of the arcades on either side of Main

Some Don'ts
● No alcohol is allowed within the theme park, nor are guests allowed to bring their own food. A picnic area is located between Guest Parking and the Main Entrance.
● No pets are allowed to enter. They may be left at the Animal Care Center near the car park on production of a certificate of health, or verification of vaccination.
● Shoes and shirts must be worn at all times.
● No flash photography or video cameras are allowed inside covered attractions.
● No smoking is allowed inside attractions, or in indoor waiting areas and queues. Restaurants are divided into smoking and non-smoking sections.

Street. When you get to Central Plaza, at the far end of Main Street, you have a choice. To your left lie **Frontierland** and **Adventureland**, an action-packed zone which takes a good few hours to explore; to the right is the futuristic **Discoveryland**. Straight ahead is the castle and, beyond it, **Fantasyland**.

General Guidelines
In this book, attractions are given ratings – from 1 to 3 stars. A tick used in conjunction with

Intergalactic enthusiasts adore Star Tours in Discoveryland

And some Dos

- Remember to bring along a sweater and some light rainwear, and put on comfortable shoes. Sun protection may be necessary in summer.
- If you are a hotel guest, pack a swimsuit.
- Bring your camera.
- Remember in which section of the car park you leave your vehicle.
- Children under seven must be accompanied by an adult.
- Get a hand-stamp if you leave the theme park so that you can get back in again later, and make sure you have your Euro Disneyland passport with you.
- Check what time the theme park closes.
- Pick up an **Entertainment Program**, giving the times of shows, from City Hall in Main Street, U.S.A..
- Visit the tourist office at Festival Disney if you are thinking about touring outside the theme park (tel: 60 43 33 33).
- Life is easier if you have a credit card with you (American Express, Visa/Barclaycard or Access/Mastercard). (If you are staying at a Euro Disney hotel, you will be given a chargecard which you can use within the theme park.)

the star rating indicates an attraction that is considered to be one of the 'top ten' in the Resort. (See also page 3.) Every ride is someone's favourite, and someone else's least favourite. You will not know if you like something unless you try it, so try not to prejudge anything. Have a go. Information about opening times, operating procedures and so on is subject to change without notice, and it is always advisable to check with Guest Relations if you have any particular requirements (tel: 64 74 30 00).

THEME PARK TIPS

Charges

The prices quoted below are intended to serve as a guide only, and were current *at the time of going to press.* Exact prices should be checked with Euro Disney at the time of your visit. (F = French franc.)

One-day Passport Adults F225; Children F150

Two-day Passport Adults F425; Children F285

Three-day Passport Adults F565; Children F375

Annual Passport Adults F990; Children F660

Car Parking F30 per day

Shuttle Buses Airport buses: F65 (single fare)

RER From central Paris: F31 (single fare)

Pets The Animal Care Center charges F45 per day (including food), or F65 overnight.

Left-luggage lockers F10 per use.

Wheelchair or stroller rental F30 per day, plus F20 refundable deposit.

Buffalo Bill's Wild West Show (Festival Disney) Adults F300; children F200 (drinks and dinner included).

Resort Hotels Room prices vary according to season and category of hotel: in summer 1992 from F550 to F1,950; low season F450 to F1,300 (most bedrooms sleep families of four). (Some hotels may open on a seasonal basis.)

Camp Davy Crockett F875 (summer), F575 (low season) per night for a luxury trailer cabin (sleeping six); pitches for tents, caravans and campervans, F270 all year round.

Games arcades Electronic machines in the hotels, campground and at Festival Disney take F5 or F10 pieces.

Euro Disneyland Passports

Entrance tickets to the theme park are called 'passports' in Disney parlance, to give that extra boost to the illusion that you really are travelling across a frontier into Wonderland. There are two tiers of charges: one for children aged between three and eleven (child passport), and one for anyone aged twelve or over (adult passport). Children under three enter free of charge. In addition, you can buy a passport for one, two, or three days (the extended passports are cheaper pro rata than one-

Scanning a Passport

Main Street Station

All aboard, please!
The **Euro Disneyland Railroad** train, compos
authentic steam locomotive, sets out from M
taining ride round Euro Disneyland theme pa
and **Fantasyland**.
En route, a five-tableau **diorama** depicts the n
life of the American **Grand Canyon**.

Harmony Barber

problem for
tilt-back ch
or haircut.

mark
pear
int.

eve world in the heart of Euro Disn
an fairy tales (Grimm, Perrault and Carr
ated classics, inhabits this quaint village w.
European countries. You may run across p
ow White, Captain Hook and well-known Dis
Mouse, Minnie Mouse, Pluto and Donald Duc
ose for souvenir photos.

day passports; they do not have
to be used on consecutive
days). Annual passports are
also available. Entrance
charges are subject to constant
revision (not necessarily
upwards, either – Disney is well
aware of market forces).Your
passport entitles you to free and
unlimited use of any of the
attractions within the theme
park during operating hours,

Tickets to ride

except the **Rustler Roundup
Shootin' Gallery** (F10 a go –
1992 price). Occasionally
attractions may be closed for
technical reasons (such as
safety checks).

Opening Times
For full details, see the
Directory section on page 118.

Planning Your Visit

Your action plan depends very much on what sort of ticket you have. If you have bought just a one-day passport, you will have to tackle Euro Disneyland Park like a military exercise if you want to see it all. Get there early (at least half an hour before the official opening time) and prepare for a fairly gruelling day. Head for the popular rides first (**Big Thunder Mountain** or **Star Tours**), and make the most of slack periods (during French mealtimes, for example, or in the evening). You will obviously get more value out of your ticket if you choose a time when the Park stays open late (in summer, or at peak holiday times).

If you have small children, subjecting them to a route march may be stressful. They

Festival Disney comes alive when the theme park closes

consecutive days. If you are staying at Euro Disney Resort for several days, it is a good idea to have a break from the Park at some point to get in touch with reality again – tour an area of France, or go to Paris. Then come back and have another day. Most people can have a good two days' fun out of Euro Disneyland Park; keen theme-parkers, or regular visitors to France, like to stay even longer. What if you hate it once you get inside? Well, it is true that not everyone likes theme parks. The chances are, though, that you will want more time than you actually have available at the Park.

If you do buy a multiple-day ticket, do not try to see the whole of the Park on Day One. Save some of the excitement for

(or you) will probably run out of stamina before seeing everything, and that is frustrating. It is much more relaxing to take the Park gradually, over two or three days. That way, you can take a rest whenever you like, and do the things you like best more than once. Two- or three-day passports are more economical than single-day passports, and you do not have to use them on

---

Quick Visits

If you have only one day, or just want a rapid tour of the theme park, these are the things you should definitely catch (but see **Contra-indications** on page 31).
Le Château de la Belle au Bois Dormant (Sleeping Beauty's Castle)
La Tanière du Dragon (the Dragon's Lair)
Big Thunder Mountain
Phantom Manor
Pirates of the Caribbean
Star Tours
Main Street Electrical Parade and **Les Feux du Château** (fireworks display). Seasonal basis only.

your next visit. Visit Main Street U.S.A., the castle, Fantasyland and Discoveryland on Day One, and then go to Frontierland and Adventureland on Day Two. You can try out your favourite rides again, have a relaxing lunch, look round all the shops, or even leave the Park for a nap or a swim at your hotel, if you like, on Day Three. Here is a brief run-down of attractions, showing which ones are best for which people, bearing in mind that there is something for everyone in each of the lands. (See also **Children,** page 104.)

Young Children
Very young children will enjoy the rides on **Main Street**, the **Château de la Belle au Bois Dormant** (Sleeping Beauty's Castle) and **Fantasyland** best. Take them for a gentle boat ride round the **Rivers of the Far West**, and visit **Critter Corral** to see some real live animals. Make sure they get a chance to meet **Mickey Mouse** at some point, too. They will probably enjoy **La Cabane des Robinson** (the Swiss Family Robinson Treehouse) and the **Pirates of the Caribbean**. See the shows at **Fantasy Festival Stage** or **Le Théâtre du Château** (the Castle Theatre). Also, catch at least the daytime parade, even if you do not want to keep the children up late enough to see Main Street Electrical Parade.

Older Children
Boys usually prefer **Frontierland**, **Adventureland**, and **Discoveryland**, so go to them when you have seen the castle. After a few rides they

may want to try absolutely everything, even 'baby rides' like **Dumbo the Flying Elephant** and **Le Carrousel de Lancelot** (Lancelot's Carousel), but they may scorn **Fantasyland's** younger appeal at first.

A Spot of Adrenalin
Frontierland attractions include a journey on a runaway mine train at **Big Thunder Mountain** and a visit to **Phantom Manor**. Also have a go shooting bank robbers at the **Rustler Roundup Shootin' Gallery** (you will need some extra francs for this), and watch out for the sheriff and his deputy tackling a bunch of bank robbers across the rooftops of **The Lucky Nugget Saloon**. In Adventureland try the rope and plank bridges, and **Teetering Rock**. In Discoveryland go for maximum throttle in a 'car of the future' on **Autopia** (the race-track), or pilot a spaceship in **Orbitron**. Best of all is **Star Tours**, a ride through outer space combining technology and sound effects. In the evening, be sure to catch the fireworks (seasonal basis only). The last few seconds are extremely exciting. (See also **Contra-indications** on page 31.)

Gentle Attractions
Start with a trip in one of the vehicles in Main Street, perhaps that nice **Horse-Drawn Streetcar**. At **Central Plaza**, keep going for the castle. Do not miss the **magic polage window**, which changes design as you look at it, and the tapestries and stained glass

upstairs in the gallery. In
Fantasyland beyond, **Le
Carrousel de Lancelot**
(Lancelot's Carousel), an old-
fashioned fairground ride with
bobbing medieval horses, is a
must. After that you could try
any of the fairytale theme rides:
Peter Pan, **Les Voyages de
Pinocchio** (Pinocchio's
Travels), or **Blanche-Neige et
les Sept Nains** (Snow White
and the Seven Dwarfs). Try
your luck with **Alice's Curious
Labyrinth** (mind the Queen of
Hearts), and **It's a Small World**.
In Adventureland, see **La
Cabane des Robinson** (the
Swiss Family Robinson
Treehouse). In Frontierland,
take a lazy trip on a
paddlewheel steamboat or

keelboat round the **Rivers of
the Far West**. A trip on the **Euro
Disneyland Railroad** is a nice
way to finish.

Contra-indications
● Several of the rides have age
restrictions (no children under
three on **Big Thunder Mountain**
and **Star Tours**; none under one
on **Dumbo the Flying
Elephant**, **Obitron** and
Autopia). There are minimum
height requirements for
passengers on rides such as
Big Thunder Mountain and
Autopia, and children under
seven are not allowed to ride on
any attraction unaccompanied.
● If you suffer from motion

*Colourful maps direct visitors to
the theme park*

THEME PARK TIPS

sickness you may be better off avoiding **Big Thunder Mountain**, **Star Tours**, or whirling rides like **Orbitron** and the **Mad Hatter's Tea Cups**, though an excess of ice cream is usually more to blame for queasiness than the rides themselves. **Le Visionarium** can also be mildly disturbing.

The pictures on the screen give a very convincing illusion of motion. **Captain EO** is extremely loud and intense.
● If you are pregnant, or have a weak back, heart or neck, avoid jolting rides.

Fun for everyone at Main Street Parade

What to See

The Essential rating system:

| ✓ | 'top ten' |

◆◆◆ do not miss
◆◆   see if you can
◆   worth seeing if
     you have time

MAIN STREET, U.S.A.

The scene is set by the
flamboyant Victorian splendour
of the **Disneyland Hotel**
straddling the entrance gates,
even before you pass through
the turnstiles into **Station Plaza**.
Once visitors emerge into
Town Square from **Main Street
Station**, they are in small-town
America at about the turn of the
century (as those of us who
never saw it like to imagine it
might have been). It is a world
of gas-lamps and horse-drawn
streetcars, decorative lettering
and absurdly pretty
architecture, all in the colours of
Italian ice cream. Each minutely
detailed façade in Town Square
and Main Street is different, but
the ornate balustrades and
barge boards, pediments and
parapets seem to be in perfect
scale and harmony. This is a
magnificent piece of deception
by the Disney Imagineers – the
top storeys are subtly
graduated in size, so that the
castle appears much further
away than it really is. All the
street furniture – lamp-posts,
letter-boxes, litter-bins, fire
hydrants – have been carefully

Travel by horse-drawn streetcar

designed to suit the period.
Main Street, U.S.A. is the
orientation centre of the Park,
where you can ask for
information, store belongings,
hire wheelchairs or pushchairs,
book guided tours, find out
about lost property (or lost
people), and generally warm to
the Disney mood as marching

bands, saxophone quintets and other entertainers keep up a brisk tempo. The rest of Main Street is mostly devoted to shops and eating places, all American style. In **Town Square** there are neat municipal gardens, park benches and a gazebo, where you can wait for one of the trundling period vehicles to take you down Main Street. Main Street links Town Square with the hub of the theme park, **Central Plaza**, beside which **Le Château de la Belle au Bois Dormant** (Sleeping Beauty's Castle) stands. From here you can choose which of the lands to see next. If you prefer, you can take a train from Main Street Station, located up steps just inside Town Square, and either go on a complete train circuit of the Park to get your bearings, or get off at Frontierland or Fantasyland.

Main Street, U.S.A. is popular with vehicle enthusiasts

WHAT TO SEE

◆
ARCADES
There are two covered passageways on either side of Main Street, with rear access to the shops and restaurants. Inside they are beautifully decorated in *fin-de-siècle* style, with wrought-iron work and pretty gas lamps. **Liberty Arcade**, on the left side of Main Street as you face the castle, contains an exhibition about the Statue of Liberty, with plans, drawings, photographs and the **Statue of Liberty Tableau**. This is a diorama about the unveiling of the monument – a diplomatic touch by Disney, emphasising Franco-American friendship and collaboration. **Discovery Arcade**, on the right side of Main Street, has cabinets showing various inventions – flying machines, strange sporting equipment and so on. Fun to look at if you have lots of time.

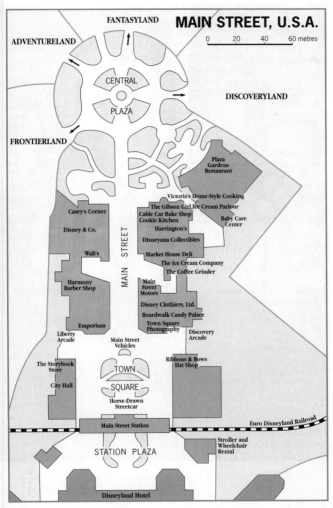

MAIN STREET, U.S.A.

FANTASYLAND

ADVENTURELAND

CENTRAL

PLAZA

DISCOVERYLAND

FRONTIERLAND

0   20   40   60 metres

Plaza
Gardens
Restaurant

Victoria's Home-Style Cooking

The Gibson Girl Ice Cream Parlour

Casey's Corner

Cable Car Bake Shop
Cookie Kitchen

Baby Care
Center

Disney & Co.

Harrington's

Disneyana Collectibles

Walt's

Market House Deli

The Ice Cream Company

MAIN STREET

The Coffee Grinder

Harmony
Barber Shop

Main
Street
Motors

Disney Clothiers, Ltd.

Emporium

Boardwalk Candy Palace

Town Square
Photography

Discovery
Arcade

Liberty
Arcade

Main Street
Vehicles

The Storybook
Store

TOWN

Ribbons & Bows
Hat Shop

City Hall

SQUARE

Horse-Drawn
Streetcar

Euro Disneyland Railroad

Main Street Station

STATION PLAZA

Stroller and
Wheelchair
Rental

Disneyland Hotel

◆◆

EURO DISNEYLAND RAILROAD

These charming steam engines chug around the perimeter of the Park, stopping at two other stations: **Frontierland Depot** and **Fantasyland Station**. No Disney theme park would be complete without an old train or two, for nostalgic railways were one of Walt's abiding passions.

At Euro Disneyland Park there are three individual, authentically styled locomotives, all beautifully painted and fitted and evoking the great railroad days of late-19th-century America. One is a **Presidential Train** of the type used by government officials, another a pioneering **Wild West Train**, the third an **East Coast Excursion Train**. The engines were manufactured by Welsh boilermakers with every detail carefully in place: whistles, smoke-stacks, cowcatchers and shiny brass fittings. The carriages (five

attached to each engine) are
open on one side, giving good
views of the Park. Each train
can take about 270 passengers,
and one arrives every 10
minutes or so. The station-
master regales passengers with
instructions over a loudspeaker
as they wait.

*If you prefer buses to trains, take
a trip down Memory Lane on a
Main Street omnibus*

On the journey between Main
Street Station and Frontierland
Depot the train passes through
Grand Canyon Diorama (see
page 45).

◆◆◆
LA PARADE DISNEY AND MAIN STREET ELECTRICAL PARADE ✓

The Disney parades are a major attraction and a real focal point of Main Street. They are elaborate, colourful spectacles like carnival processions, with lots of floats. They start near Fantasyland and proceed down Main Street.

Tips
● If there is anything you do not want to take around the Park with you, leave it in the coin-operated lockers beneath Main Street Station (charge F10).
● If you are particularly keen to see any attraction, restaurant or show, check at City Hall that it is available.
● Riding a streetcar is a good way of avoiding temptation in **Boardwalk Candy Palace**.
● Do not become mesmerised by all the shops and balloon-sellers unless you have plenty of time. If you spend too long on them, you will not have time to see the rest of the Park.
● Do not let children eat too many sweets before they go on rides.
● If it is raining, head for the arcades at either side of Main Street.
● You can steal a march on the queues by arriving early and walking from Main Street to **Frontierland**. Then head for popular attractions before everyone else arrives.

The colourful spectacle of La Parade Disney

You will find the area very crowded. Stake out a good vantage point in advance. If you time a visit to **Walt's – an American Restaurant** very carefully and are lucky enough to get a window table (very expensive, though) you should get a good view of the parades from the upper floor. Views from the other Main Street restaurants are distant, or will probably be blocked by kerb-side spectators, but you may be lucky in Plaza Gardens. **La Parade Disney**, usually at 15.00 or 16.00hrs, contains a cast of over 200 costumed characters including Mickey Mouse and his friends. The 12 great floats depict fairytale scenes from *Pinocchio*, *Peter Pan*, *Sleeping Beauty* and *The Little Mermaid*. One of the best is of Cinderella in her pumpkin coach, flamboyantly driven by a handsome coachman, who looks a bit like Mozart. Clowns, jugglers and marching bands compete with the formidable battery of sound systems relaying the Prague Symphony Orchestra, playing the specially commissioned score. By night the spectacle is even more remarkable. The **Main Street Electrical Parade**, adopted from Disney theme parks in America, contains over 700,000 light bulbs, winking and glowing as night falls in the Park. This parade is definitely worth catching. It has twice as many floats as La Parade Disney, and some wonderful creations. Alice sits on top of

*Main Street Electrical Parade
in all its glory*

her magic mushroom, and Elliot, a docile dragon, snorts steam at admirers. There are also some delightful twirling snails.

As if all this is not enough, the evening's entertainment sometimes ends with a remarkable fireworks display. Guests should note that both the Main Street Electrical Parade and fireworks display are seasonal only.

◆
VEHICLES

Other modes of transportation available in Main Street date from the same era as the trains. These vehicles are not genuine antiques, but they are authentically recreated by master craftsmen. Among them are **Horse-Drawn Streetcars** pulled by patient Shires and Percherons (a nod to the French here – it is a local breed), an early double-decker **Omnibus**, a chauffeured **Limousine**, a **Fire Truck** and a police **Paddy Wagon**. Guests can queue up in Town Square for a brief ride to Central Plaza in whichever of these vehicles is running. At **Main Street Motors** you can also find some genuine reconditioned vintage motor cars. You can even drive one of these vehicles away; they are all for sale (at $75,000 or so).

FRONTIERLAND

This is the largest of the five lands, distinguished from the others by a Wild West theme, large expanses of water, and a spectacular man-made Arizona landscape. Here there is arguably the Park's most exciting attraction, **Big Thunder Mountain**, and three different kinds of boat trip are offered. Like Main Street, U.S.A., Frontierland has a clear architectural theme, based on an imaginary Wild West town of the late 1800s called Thunder Mesa. If parts of Frontierland look surprisingly authentic, that is because they are. Disney Imagineers collected real antiques from many states in the US, and transported them here for special effect.

There is something for everyone at Frontierland. Even if you are not a Wild West enthusiast, you will almost certainly be impressed by the drama of this entirely artificial landscape, created from flat, unpromising terrain.

You can approach Frontierland from several directions. The

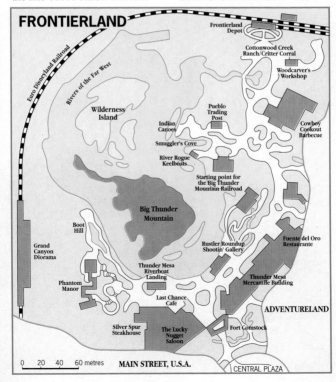

FRONTIERLAND

Tips

- If it is raining you can walk under cover to Frontierland, from Liberty Arcade in Main Street, or from the Adventureland Bazar.
- **Big Thunder Mountain** and (to a lesser extent) **Phantom Manor** are major attractions where queues are likely to be long, so try to visit them early, late, or at meal or parade times.
- If the weather is hot, head for the paddlewheel steamboats or River Rogue Keelboats.

usual way is from Central Plaza, through **Fort Comstock**, the log stockade. If you are going around the Park anti-clockwise, you can approach Frontierland from Adventureland, and watch how cleverly the pirate scene fades to cowboys and Indians. You can also come by train (they chug clockwise round the Park). On the way between Main Street Station and Frontierland Depot, trains pass through **Grand Canyon Diorama**.

Big Thunder Mountain is at the heart of Frontierland

WHAT TO SEE

◆◆◆
BIG THUNDER MOUNTAIN ✓

The most exciting and conspicuous attraction in Frontierland, and certainly one of the best in the Park. It may take a little while to pluck up enough courage to visit it, so wild are the screams. But do not miss it. It is reached by taking a roller-coaster ride aboard a runaway mine train. The track passes through a carefully reconstructed landscape, similar to that found in Arizona or Utah, particularly around Monument Valley. The rocky set rises to 119 feet (36m), and immense pains have been taken to achieve an impression of age in the mine buildings, by means of staining, bleaching and rusting.

The ride is certainly wilder than at Orlando. What makes the former so good is its mystery factor. With most roller-coasters you can see exactly what happens: they go up, they go down, your stomach arrives sometime afterwards, everybody screams. But with the runaway roller-coaster at

FRONTIERLAND

Big Thunder Mountain, nobody can predict what will happen once the train goes into the mine-workings.

Even the queuing is creative for this attraction – which is just as well because there will probably be plenty of it. The tightly coiled lines shuffle steadily through the headquarters and assay office

The runaway mine train is not for the faint-hearted!

of the Big Thunder Mountain Mining Company. Pumps and milling equipment lie all around; you can peer into deserted windows and down old chutes – the set is extremely realistic. Tension builds up as the point of no return is reached. The train pulls away, then plunges into a shaft and the caverns of the mine-workings, full of stalactites and glowing bats' eyes. Hurtling through a mining camp and a pine-forest,

where opossums swing from the branches, the train then dives into a dynamite explosion. The roof caves in, briefly revealing huge veins of gold. The train plunges on, this time facing a new danger from the flooding river, which is washing away part of the track. Eventually the exhilarated passengers are brought safely back to base, chortling with delight.

It is difficult to take in all the details of the attraction in one go; there are all kinds of things that you will miss first time round. This is certainly one attraction that can stand a repeat performance, if you can bear the queuing. Children under three (or below a certain height) are not allowed to go on the ride; nor should anyone consider going on it if they are pregnant, or have neck or back problems.

COTTONWOOD CREEK RANCH

A typical Western ranch near Frontierland Depot (railway station). In **Critter Corral** visitors can see and pet some real animals of an unthreatening sort.

◆

FORT COMSTOCK

This fort, at the main entrance to Frontierland, is a replica of the sort of log stockade constructed by early pioneers as a defence against Indian attack. You can climb the lookout tower to the telescopes on the upper level and gaze over Central Plaza. At night the stockade doors are lit by torches.

◆

GRAND CANYON DIORAMA

Although located within Frontierland, this atraction can only be seen from the **Euro Disneyland Railroad** (trains depart from Main Street, Frontierland and Fantasyland Stations).

Trains enter a 262-foot (80-m) tunnel, in which the scenery of the Grand Canyon is recreated, subtly lit as though the journey along the canyon rim takes not just a few minutes, but an entire day from sunrise to sunset. Guests first encounter ancient Indian cliff dwellings hollowed from the canyon walls, and then a forest in which a herd of deer is grazing. Other wildlife can be seen, too: a fox stalking a pack rat; a rattlesnake coiled on a ledge; raccoons and squirrels; and a cougar and her cubs by a cave. A thunderstorm gathers and as a rainbow forms, antelope descend into the canyon. The diorama consists of a huge mural, with many animals and species of vegetation. Lighting, music and sound effects all play a part. As the train emerges from the tunnel passengers find they have reached the **Rivers of the Far West**, with **Big Thunder Mountain** beyond.

◆◆

INDIAN CANOES

Disney guests form surprisingly long queues for this attraction, apparently keen on the idea of doing their own paddling. The canoes leave until dusk from a dock near **Pueblo Trading Post**. The voyage time depends on how energetic the crew is.

FRONTIERLAND

◆◆◆
PHANTOM MANOR ✓

The eerie, ramshackle mansion of Phantom Manor was built by one of Thunder Mesa's early settlers, who became rich during the Gold Rush. But tragedy struck when his only daughter disappeared on her wedding day. The house was left empty and fell into decay. You can believe this if you like – but isn't that a candle inside? Guests bound for Phantom Manor are ushered into a strange circular room by sinister hosts. The doors shut and the walls change shape. Those innocent-looking pictures take on horrifying new dimensions as the floor stretches. Guests then descend to board a 'Doom Buggy' for the journey through the house. Mocking laughter, beating door-knockers, creaking

*All sorts of spooks haunt
Phantom Manor*

hinges, and a clock tolling 13 start the mystery tour. A ghostly bride appears sobbing at intervals, while a medium's head is visible in a crystal ball. One of the best special effects is the holograms, which are used for the wedding feast. Guests dance and fade, and a parade of ghosts, ghouls and skeletons follows before the passengers are released from their ordeal.

Outside in the fresh air, guests emerge near **Boot Hill**, the cemetery overlooking the Rivers of the Far West, which is full of amusing gravestones. Some are even, by Disney standards, slightly *risqué*: 'Sacred to the Memory of Rev. Jared Bates, who died Aug 6 1862. Erected by the girls of The Lucky Nugget Saloon ...'.

◆◆
RIVER ROGUE KEELBOATS (RACCOON AND COYOTE)

These boats are modelled on the ones used in a Disney television film called *Davy Crockett and the River Pirates*. They are diesel-powered, 40 feet (12m) long and hold about 40 passengers each. Unlike the stately paddlewheel riverboats, which follow a fixed course, the keelboats weave in and out, and you may find yourself perilously close to the rocks at some point. The keelboats leave from a dock at **Smuggler's Cove**.

*Stately paddlewheel riverboats
like the Mark Twain (right) vie
for trade with canoes on the
Rivers of the Far West*

FRONTIERLAND

◆
RUSTLER ROUNDUP SHOOTIN' GALLERY

This is fun. Instead of bullets, the guns fire electronic impulses at a Wild West scene containing 74 animated targets: among them cacti, a windmill and a dynamite shack. (The only human one is a peeping Tom.) If you hit them, all kinds of things happen. There is a charge for this attraction to prevent people from hogging the guns all day.

◆◆
THUNDER MESA RIVERBOAT LANDING (PADDLEWHEEL RIVERBOATS)

The careful landscaping and detailing of the various sections of the **Rivers of the Far West** make the paddlewheel riverboat trip round **Big Thunder Mountain** quite an adventure. On the way you will see **Smuggler's Cove**; **Wilderness Island**, a green oasis where Joe sleeps in a rocking-chair, his dog barking at passing boats; **Settlers' Landing**, a dry dock with supplies for pioneering homesteaders; an abandoned wagon with two skeletal oxen in the sand; and **Geyser Plateau**, where steaming, bubbling, mineral-rich water jets over the bones of dinosaurs. The scenery evokes the landscape of the Wild West, with its grand geological formations (rock bridges and canyons) and high desert plateaux known as *mesas*.

From Thunder Mesa Riverboat Landing near the **Silver Spur Steakhouse** visitors can choose

Boot Hill, a place of rest in Frontierland

between two riverboats: *Mark Twain* and *Molly Brown*. They are authentically reconstructed paddlewheel riverboats of the type that plied the Mississippi and Sacramento rivers at the time of the Gold Rush. One is a stern-wheeler, the other a side-wheeler. They were both built for Euro Disneyland Park. The vessels are ornately fitted with mahogany and brass, with teak decks and comfortable upholstery. Each boat carries about 400 passengers, and their nostalgic voyage lasts around 15 minutes.

ADVENTURELAND

Adventureland is one of the most attractive parts of the theme park. Pleasantly landscaped in a natural style, it has water, islands, rocks and lots of vegetation, including a bamboo grove. In addition, it has one of the best and most popular rides, a collection of genuinely interesting shops in its North African bazar, and several of the nicest eating places. In all, it has a lot going for it, and should appeal to any age group. The main attraction, **Pirates of the Caribbean**, is complex and technically sophisticated – yet

Adventureland as a whole has an air of innocence about it in keeping with the original spirit of Disney. Its pleasures are simpler than much of the Park – climbing treehouses, walking wobbly bridges, exploring caves. The central physical feature of Adventureland is **Adventure Isle**, a moated double-island connected by two exciting bridges. Skilful landscaping gives this area the impression of being larger than it really is. Elements from three well-known Disney movies are incorporated into the themes here: *Peter Pan*, *Treasure Island* and *Swiss Family Robinson*.

ADVENTURELAND

- Blue Lagoon Restaurant
- Explorers Club Restaurant
- Pirates of the Caribbean
- The Shipwreck
- Ben Gunn's Cave
- Le Coffre du Capitaine
- Spyglass Hill
- Adventure Isle
- Skull Rock
- La Cabane des Robinson
- Le Ventre de la Terre
- Captain Hook's Pirate Ship
- Trader Sam's Jungle Boutique
- Café de la Brousse
- Le Chant des Tam-Tams
- La Reine des Serpents
- Aux Epices Enchantées
- Les Trésors de Schéhérazade
- L'Echoppe d'Aladin
- La Girafe Curieuse
- FRONTIERLAND
- FANTASYLAND
- Adventureland Bazar
- 0 20 40 60 metres
- CENTRAL PLAZA

WHAT TO SEE

◆◆

ADVENTURE ISLE

The north section of Adventure Isle is given over to a pirate theme. The Jolly Roger flies by the lookout tower on **Spyglass Hill**. Below is **Ben Gunn's Cave**, with six different entrances: **Dead Man's Maze**, **Davy Jones's Locker**, and so on, leading to mysterious passages haunted by bats and skeletons. Waterfalls hurtle past gaps in the rock. If you look at the rock carefully, you will see that it is shaped like an enormous skull. **Captain Hook's Pirate Ship** is moored in the cove nearby, and you can walk over the top deck to spy out the land. Down below, light snacks are served from the galley. At night **Skull Rock** and the waterfalls are illuminated. They look most eerie.

◆◆

LA CABANE DES ROBINSON (THE SWISS FAMILY ROBINSON TREEHOUSE)

Prominent on **Adventure Isle** is a strange-looking banyan (fig) tree, rising 91 feet (28m). In its branches is the ultimate treehouse, where the resourceful Robinson family have made a home from shipwrecked timbers. You climb the hand-made stairs into the branches of the tree, past an ingenious device of bamboo cups and rope pulleys for carrying water round the house. Wooden stairways lead to various rooms – a library and kitchen downstairs, a family room with a hand-pumped organ, and bedrooms on the

> **Tip**
> ● The **Adventureland Bazar** is an interesting place to shop, and a good place to get out of rain or sun.

upper levels. Quaint, homely texts are carefully placed around the house. Down by the roots of the tree is **le Ventre de la Terre**, where supplies from the wreck are stored behind bamboo bars. (The actual wreck can be seen under the suspended bridge.) The tree is artificial, with 300,000 leaves and 50,000 flowers. The attraction also contains over 950 separate props, mostly replicas.

♦♦♦ PIRATES OF THE CARIBBEAN

One of the block-busting attractions of the park, a must for everyone. There are similar attractions at the other Disney theme parks, too, but here the latest *Audio-Animatronics®* technology is employed, giving an even wider range of special effects. As you make your way through the rocky grotto to the boats, you can hear roistering buccaneers singing their favourite song. You are about to embark on a time-travel

Crossing to Adventure Isle

adventure, going back to a 17th-century scene somewhere in the West Indies, where palms wave and the air is warm and balmy. The boat sets off through the moonlit **Blue Lagoon** and floats alongside a shipwreck, where an octopus and a crab curiously inspect some sunken treasure. Gradually the sounds of distant gunfire grow louder; a fortress is being shelled by a pirate ship. Pirates are attempting to scale the walls, daggers clutched between their teeth. The boat then passes inside the fortress. The prisoners in the dungeons call for help, and several try to entice a dog with keys in its mouth to approach

ADVENTURELAND

the bars. Suddenly, the boat plunges down a waterfall and returns to the battle scene. Cannon balls and smoke are everywhere. The voyage continues through the centre of a Caribbean town, and here the ride is so packed with detailed scenery that it is hard to take everything in. The mayor is a prisoner of the pirates, who are dipping him in the well to force him to reveal where the treasure is. The women are getting plenty of attention too: several pirates are bidding for fair damsels in an auction. Meanwhile, an old woman chases a pirate with a broom. Other pirates have managed by some good fortune to discover where alcohol is kept in Euro Disneyland Park (a secret denied to the rest of us) and are merrily carousing. Plunder and mayhem continue (none of it

Pirate enthusiasts can eat lunch on Captain Hook's Galley

frightening or violent). The fort's burning arsenal explodes, propelling passengers back to the present and the final stage of the ride. Passengers can buy pirate souvenirs afterwards in **Le Coffre du Capitaine**. As many as 124 *Audio-Animatronics*® figures are used, including animals. Some of the animated scenes are highly naturalistic and sophisticated: full of sword-fights, facial gestures and so on. The weapons are authentic replicas of 16th- and 17th-century pieces. The dialogue is mostly in colloquial French, but clues are almost entirely visual, so there is no great loss of enjoyment. This ride is so action-packed that you could certainly do it more than once.

FANTASYLAND

When you reach the neat gardens and fountains of Central Plaza, you have a tricky choice: you could head for the Wild West of Frontierland, the exotic Islamic domes of Adventureland, or the futuristic whirling globes of Discoveryland's Orbitron. Straight ahead of you, however, stands an irresistible invitation: the mysterious gilded pinnacles of a truly fantastic castle, and the drawbridge is down, just waiting for you to cross. So why fight it? You will have to visit it at some point. Le Château de la

Belle au Bois Dormant (Sleeping Beauty's Castle), is the main landmark of Euro Disneyland Park. It is slap in the centre and unmissable, so it is always a good place to meet. As the spires can be seen from most sections of the Park, they can give bearings if you get lost.

Most of Fantasyland's attractions are designed for younger guests; teenagers may find **Dumbo the Flying Elephant** a little beneath their dignity. At first, that is. Give almost anyone a few hours in the Park, and dignity is thrown to the winds.

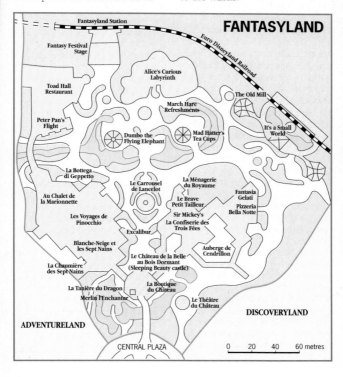

FANTASYLAND

Fantasyland Station

Euro Disneyland Railroad

Fantasy Festival Stage

Alice's Curious Labyrinth

Toad Hall Restaurant

The Old Mill

March Hare Refreshments

Peter Pan's Flight

It's a Small World

Dumbo the Flying Elephant

Mad Hatter's Tea Cups

La Bottega di Geppetto

Le Carrousel de Lancelot

La Ménagerie du Royaume

Au Chalet de la Marionnette

Le Brave Petit Tailleur

Fantasia Gelati

Sir Mickey's

Pizzeria Bella Notte

Les Voyages de Pinocchio

La Confiserie des Trois Fées

Excalibur

Blanche-Neige et les Sept Nains

Le Château de la Belle au Bois Dormant (Sleeping Beauty castle)

Auberge de Cendrillon

La Chaumière des Sept Nains

La Tanière du Dragon

La Boutique du Château

Merlin l'Enchanteur

Le Théâtre du Château

DISCOVERYLAND

ADVENTURELAND

CENTRAL PLAZA

0   20   40   60 metres

FANTASYLAND

The theme of Fantasyland, as its name suggests, is the world of fairytales: witches and dwarfs, princes and princesses, gingerbread houses and magic wishing wells. The European origin of these fairytales is heavily emphasised – Disney is ever-conscious of the host country's sensibilities. Architecture ranges from quaint, Bavarian-looking cottages to the ambitious medieval whimsy of the castle. Several of the attractions are similar in type: short rides through enclosed spaces, during which a fairy story is unfurled with many elaborate sets and moving figures. The characters are deliberately based on Disney animated films. There is no attempt to make them look like 'real people', though the advanced technology would be quite capable of doing this. From its unthreatening beginnings, each plot becomes darker before ending happily ever after. **Les Voyages de Pinocchio** (Pinocchio's Travels) or **Peter Pan's Flight** are difficult to follow if you are not already familiar with the stories, as there is little time to explain anything on the way (though you can still enjoy the rides). Queues for these attractions are lengthy, weaving back and forth through a concertina of ropes and railings.

Other attractions are of the fairground variety – in the form of classic merry-go-rounds and a few mild G-forces. If you know other Disney theme parks you will probably remember the block-busting and eternally popular **It's a Small World**, here given more elaboration. A completely new attraction is the hedge maze of **Alice's Curious Labyrinth** – again, a strongly European feature. Elsewhere in Fantasyland there are many shops selling toys and sweets, and there are also lots of fairytale eating places (designed mostly with children in mind), including the only restaurant in the Park with French cuisine. You can reach Fantasyland by the **Euro Disneyland Railroad**, but after that you must use your feet.

Le Château de la Belle au Bois Dormant (Sleeping Beauty's Castle)

Tips
● Catch the fantasy attractions when queues are short, if you can – early or late in the day, or during meal-times and parades, when crowds will be thinner.
● Very young or susceptible children may find parts of **Blanche-Neige et les Sept Nains** (Snow White and the Seven Dwarfs), **La Tanière du Dragon** (The Dragon's Lair) and **Peter Pan's Flight** frightening.
● Check show times at **Le Théâtre du Château** or the **Fantasy Festival Stage** when you arrive.
● You may have an expensive time if you let your children investigate too many of the shops.
● If you have a long wait for a fairytale ride, spend time recapping the storyline; children get more out of it.

FANTASYLAND

WHAT TO SEE

Alice's Curious Labyrinth

◆◆
ALICE'S CURIOUS LABYRINTH

Based, of course, on *Alice in Wonderland*, this maze of clipped yew and ivy hedges is 1,200 feet (366m) long. The maze explorer passes characters and scenes from *Alice*: the Cheshire Cat, which rolls its eyes and twitches its tail, a blue caterpillar calmly smoking a hookah, strange birds and, of course, the choleric Queen of Hearts

advocating decapitation at every turn. Eventually you reach a small purple castle, full of optical illusions. The jumping fountains transfix passers-by; arcs of water leap from pool to pool round the edge of the maze. The designs for some parts of this attraction may seem crude (notably the Queen of Hearts and the floral Cheshire Cat), but they are unusual and keep children amused for quite some time.

◆◆
LE CARROUSEL DE LANCELOT (LANCELOT'S CAROUSEL)

A classic merry-go-round, with 86 ornate, medieval war horses galloping sedately in fairytale scenes. A gentle but enjoyable ride.

◆
BLANCHE-NEIGE ET LES SEPT NAINS (SNOW WHITE AND THE SEVEN DWARFS)

Climb aboard the diamond-mine cars outside the Dwarfs' cottage, and set off through this German fairytale, on which Walt Disney based one of his most successful animated films. The wicked queen does her stuff with the mirror and the poisoned apple, and Prince Charming appears at the end.

Pinocchio meets the crowds

FANTASYLAND

◆◆◆
LE CHÂTEAU DE LA BELLE AU BOIS DORMANT (SLEEPING BEAUTY'S CASTLE) ✓

This is the archetypal interpretation of a castle – one we instantly recognise from the pages of any storybook, or from early Disney movies, such as the animated classic *Sleeping Beauty*. The design is based on illustrations from a 17th-century edition of *Les Très Riches Heures du Duc de Berry*, and the building rises 149 feet (45.5m) above the moat. It seems much higher because a technique known as 'forced perspective' has been employed, in which stones at the top are cut smaller than those at the bottom, to give an illusion of height. The pink walls are topped by 16 whimsical turrets of subtle, sea-blue tiles. Pennants, weather vanes and golden finials adorn the roofline; creepers hang from the walls; and enticing stairways lead to the central tower. You may be disappointed to learn that visitors cannot actually enter the slender turrets, as they are purely ornamental. Visitors can enter the castle by the drawbridge, or from the side by the wishing well (**Le Puits Magique**); do not forget to wish. Once inside, turn and look up at the front window – and wait a few seconds. Magically, its design will transform from two doves into a rose. This is a 'polage window', and it works by means of a rotating filter. Inside the castle, besides fantasy architecture, are eight French tapestries (commissioned from the great *tapissiers* of Aubusson), and stained-glass windows telling the story of Sleeping Beauty. These are upstairs in the firelit gallery.

◆
DUMBO THE FLYING ELEPHANT

The long queues testify to the appeal of this simple roundabout for young children. You can control the height at which your elephant flies.

Dumbo, a star attraction

◆◆◆
IT'S A SMALL WORLD ✓

Like similar attractions at Tokyo, Orlando and Anaheim, this is a very popular and elaborate entertainment. In Euro Disneyland Park it is a fantastic amalgam of many different architectural landmarks, ranging from Big Ben to the Leaning Tower of Pisa. The set is constructed in miniature, in toy building-block style, with numerous moving parts. Every quarter of an hour a parade of animated figures troops around the base of the clocktower, and many exciting things happen before you are eventually told what time it is. Guests can board canal boats for a long ride by Disney standards, soon passing a gathering of *Audio-Animatronics*® 'children' from all parts of the globe. They wear authentic national costumes and sing in nine languages. Norwegian figure-skaters give way to leprechauns, Beefeaters, Flamenco dancers, Balinese fan-dancers, Eskimos, and the like. It is a saccharine show, but the technical effects are impressive. There are nearly 280 different figures, representing a phenomenal effort by the Disney costume department.

◆◆
MAD HATTER'S TEA CUPS
A pleasantly loony whirl in 18 giant tea cups, placed on a roundabout, resulting in a bewildering pirouette of motion. You control the speed using a steering wheel.

◆
PETER PAN'S FLIGHT
Pirate galleons 'sail' with their passengers over the rooftops of London to Never Land, giving an illusion of flight. Tinkerbell, Captain Hook and the Crocodile also appear.

◆◆◆
LA TANIÈRE DU DRAGON (THE DRAGON'S LAIR) ✓

The most exciting thing by far is not inside, but beneath the castle. Chained by the neck in a dark cave of bubbling pools and stalactites is a leathery grey dragon, wonderfully terrifying. It makes gentle snorings and twitchings, then flashes its red eyes and gives fierce roars, smoke pouring from its nostrils as any self-respecting dragon should. Its tail lashes in the water, while the wings move and claws tense. It is one of the most remarkable and sophisticated pieces of *Audio-Animatronics*® technology in the Park, and should not be missed.
You can reach the lair from the mysterious shop called **Merlin l'Enchanteur**, carved into the rock of the castle.

◆
LES VOYAGES DE PINOCCHIO (PINOCCHIO'S TRAVELS)
More scenes from the Disney animated film archives, based on the story told by Carlo Collodi. The cars pass from cheery Alpine landscapes into dangers and temptations, and then emerge back in Geppetto's shop, where the clockwork toys spring to life.

DISCOVERYLAND

This European version of Tomorrowland also looks back at the great inventors and visionaries of the past. Here, in France, Jules Verne is given a prominent role; H G Wells and Leonardo da Vinci are also featured. The concept of travel through time and space forms the theme of several of the adventures. Science fiction, special effects and speed are other elements to the fore. Whereas the attractions in Fantasyland or Main Street, U.S.A. are quite compact, here they are more spread out. There are fewer things to do and also fewer shops and restaurants, but the attractions take longer. There are three shows (**CinéMagique**, **Le Visionarium** and **Videopolis**), and three attractions you will probably have to queue for: **Star Tours**, **Autopia** and **Orbitron**.

If, as many people do, you tackle the theme park clockwise, this is the last land you will come to, and psychologically it feels as

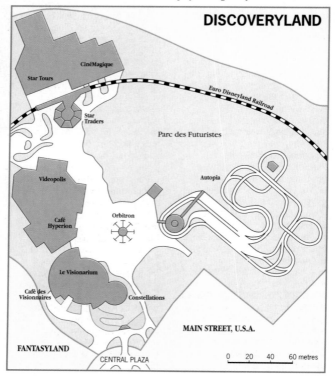

DISCOVERYLAND

CinéMagique

Star Tours

Euro Disneyland Railroad

Star Traders

Parc des Futuristes

Videopolis

Autopia

Café Hyperion

Orbitron

Le Visionarium

Café des Visionnaires

Constellations

MAIN STREET, U.S.A.

FANTASYLAND

CENTRAL PLAZA

0   20   40   60 metres

Flying on Orbitron

though it should be. The architecture is futuristic, with lights and flashing lasers. The most eye-catching attraction, clearly visible from Central Plaza, is **Orbitron**. In essence, this is a fairly simple fairground roundabout, but the design is certainly imaginative. Whirling asteroids or planets circle in opposite directions to that of the rocket-ship passenger cars, giving an added effect of speed. The whole contraption looks like something that Leonardo or Jules Verne dreamt up.

Tips
● If you feel like sitting down, time your meal at **Café Hyperion** during the **Videopolis** show.
● On **Orbitron**, remember that you can increase the thrills considerably if you take your craft to its full height by pushing the lever in front of you. The asteroids will pass much more rapidly.
● The special effects in the *Captain EO* show at **CinéMagique** are best viewed in the middle or at the back.

DISCOVERYLAND

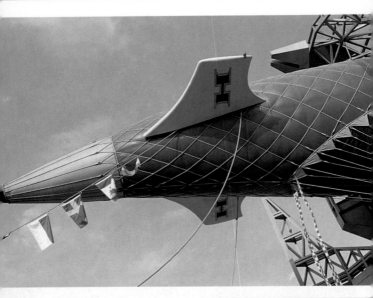

WHAT TO SEE

◆
AUTOPIA
This is a popular attraction, consisting of a ride in a 'Car of the Future' through 'Solaria', a city of tomorrow. Your car is kept firmly on a specific track, and all you have to do is press the accelerator and steer. It is actually trickier than it looks to maximise efficiency in these 50s-style vehicles equipped with special bumpers and huge exhaust pipes.

◆◆
CINÉMAGIQUE (THE MAGIC CINEMA)
Another special-effects show, already popular in other Disney theme parks. Captain EO is played by Michael Jackson. The theme is the eternal one of good versus evil, this time in a

Star Tours

sci-fi context, with lots of curious little creatures like Fuzzball the orange space monkey, or Major Domo, who turns into a drum set. The film is a 3-D show, so you have to wear special glasses to see the effects. It is shown on an enormous screen, and Angelica Huston plays the evil alien Supreme Leader. As a technical achievement, the film is certainly worth seeing.

The airship Hyperion *floats over the entrance to Videopolis*

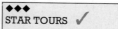

◆◆◆
STAR TOURS ✓

This exciting ride draws on the themes and special effects used in George Lucas' *Star Wars*. As much excitement is created by the build-up as by the ride itself. The sci-fi 'business' before you are actually strapped into your spacecraft, when visitors can watch friendly droids working, is all part of the fun, and certainly takes tedium out of queuing.

The ride is based on a popular comic theme: the novice driver. This one, unfortunately, is your pilot for the space flight. Fasten your seat-belts. The space craft pitches, rolls and jolts, while on-screen, rapidly moving images suggest you are falling or on some irrevocable collision course. Eventually, of course, you land safely.

◆◆
ORBITRON

There is nothing very new about the basic principle of this ride, but the look of it is certainly different. Bronze, copper and brass globes spin on various axes, the opposite way from the direction of your two-seater craft, so if you are at maximum height (controlled from inside) it seems quite fast. Queues can be long, as there are only 12 passenger vehicles.

◆◆
VIDEOPOLIS

The airship *Hyperion* marks this pavilion, which houses the **Café Hyperion** and a large tiered **auditorium**, where visitors can enjoy videos relayed on four giant screens and regularly staged live shows. These are supported by unearthly special effects created by lasers, lights and artificial mist. In the evenings when the Park is open late, Videopolis becomes a night-club.

DISCOVERYLAND

◆◆◆
LE VISIONARIUM (THE VISIONARIUM) ✓

This is an enjoyable new production based on the time-travel theme, using the medium known as *Circle-Vision 360®*, which will be familiar to anyone who has visited the Disney theme parks in America. In these attractions the audience is completely surrounded by a belt of large cinema screens. The totality of this cinematic experience is achieved by using nine different cameras controlled by computer. Spectacular landscapes, many different perspectives and a very convincing illusion of movement are just some aspects of this entertaining show. In Disney's other parks CIRCLE-VISION films have been mostly confined to tourist travelogues, but here for the first time is a plot. There is a robot inventor called Time-keeper; 9-Eye, a robot with nine cameras around her head (for this creature is female, it seems); and Jules Verne as honorary guest, collected from the Paris Exposition of 1900 for a voyage through time. Gérard Depardieu puts in a brief appearance as an airport baggage handler and Jeremy Irons as HG Wells. The shooting of this film involved some adventures, including sending the expensive nine-camera turret under the sea.

In Discoveryland you can indulge in time travel, or enjoy space travel on rides such as Orbitron (right)

EXCURSIONS FROM EURO DISNEY RESORT

EXCURSIONS FROM EURO DISNEY RESORT

Dom Perignon's name is immortalised by champagne

The plains of Brie, where Euro Disney Resort is located, are unlikely to catch the heartstrings in the way that, say, the Dordogne or the Auvergne do as holiday regions. But they are by no means devoid of interest. Historically, of course, the region is famous for its Brie cheese, those creamy flat cylinders which can be as much as 16 inches (40cm) in diameter. There are several varieties: Meaux, Coulommiers and Melun are major centres of production. Be sure to try some while you are there.

The Ile-de-France, Paris' green belt, is well known for its splendid châteaux and great forests: an hour's drive can take you to some lovely scenery. The places mentioned in this section can all be reached without negotiating too many of the Parisian ring roads.

Close by Marne-la-Vallée is the historic episcopal town of **Meaux**, famed for its mustard and garlic. Further east lies chalky **Champagne country**, and the cathedral city of **Reims**. Southwards is **Fontainebleau**, and the much smaller but exquisite château of **Vaux-le-Vicomte**. In the gentle, river-washed countryside of **Seine-et-Marne** there is the hill town of **Provins**, picturesque **Moret-sur-Loing**, and the chic artists' colony of **Barbizon**. Among many local châteaux are **Guermantes**,

Champs-sur-Marne, Fleury-en-Bière, **Ferrières** and **Chantilly**. The biggest draw of all, however, is **Paris** itself. It is beyond the scope of this book to cover the attractions of the capital, but just 40 minutes from the theme park, on an efficient suburban railway link, the city is at your feet, day or night. (See our companion guide, *Essential Paris*, for all you need to know.) Remember that many museums in central Paris are closed on Tuesdays. The tourist office in Festival Disney has plenty of information on the sights of Seine-et-Marne, and if you feel like touring the area, pick up the free leaflets here first. To see any of these places conveniently, you will definitely need a car. Car rental is available at Euro Disney Resort hotels and reservations can be made in advance (see pages 115 and 121).

◆◆
BARBIZON
37 miles (60km) southwest
A pretty woodland village with a distinguished and monied air, Barbizon's main street is now lined with smart restaurants, hotels and art galleries which make it an attractive, if not cheap, place to stay. It rose to prominence during the 1830s when a breakaway colony of landscape artists settled here to practise a style that later became known as Impressionism. **Théodore Rousseau's House** can be visited at 55 Grand-Rue; Jean-François Millet was another resident. Writers also made it their home, one house (now a

luxury hotel) being associated with Robert Louis Stevenson.

Stay or Eat:
Hostellerie la Clé d'Or, 73 Grande Rue (tel: 60 66 28 50); and **Hostellerie du Bas-Breau**, 22 Grande Rue (tel: 60 66 40 05).

◆◆
CHAMPAGNE COUNTRY
68 miles (109km) northeast
Many visitors see Reims (described in detail on page 73) through a cloud of bubbles, for most of the great champagne houses are based here in tunnels and caverns called *crayères,* hollowed out of the chalky soil on which the city – and much of the city's prosperity – stands. The hillsides south of Reims provide ideal conditions for France's most famous vineyards. Vines have flourished here since Roman times, but it was not until that cellar-master monk Dom Perignon spotted the potential of secondary fermentation that the wines of Champagne really began to sparkle in the world's eyes. Now this hugely prestigious and wealthy industry has developed a sideline to help promote its wares: tourism. Nearly all the big houses offer highly organised, guided tours, and most of them are free.
Champagne tours are now immensely popular, too, and if you want to join one on a busy weekend it is as well to book in advance. Do not be put off if the tourist office tells you they are full; just turn up and someone will fit you in. Some of the major

EXCURSIONS FROM EURO DISNEY RESORT

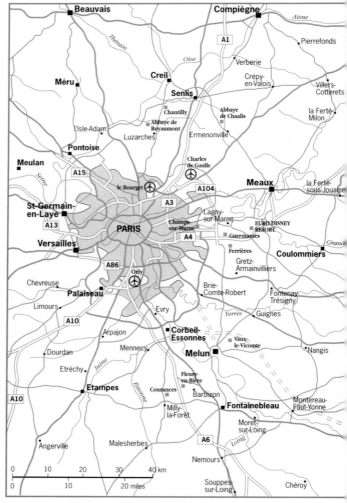

champagne houses in Reims include **Mumm**, **Piper-Heidsieck**, **Lanson**, **Taittinger**, **Ruinart**, **Veuve Cliquot-Ponsardin**, **Pommery** and **Laurent-Perrier**. Some of these offer tastings after films and explanations of champagne-making. You can also buy, of course (though there is no great pressure to do so, and no great saving on normal retail

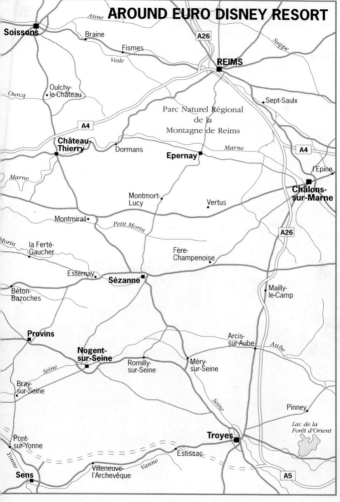

AROUND EURO DISNEY RESORT

prices in France). Do not, however, expect to troop round gorgeous, crumbly old châteaux: the champagne houses are commercial buildings – suitably imposing, but scarcely of great historic interest.

If you cannot join a champagne tour in Reims, do not despair. Head down the road to **Epernay**, a smaller capital of the champagne trade, where yet more bubbling names line the famous **Avenue du Champagne** in letters of gold: **Moët et Chandon**, **Mercier**, **Perrier-Jouet**. Both Moët and Mercier give very professional tours in several languages showing all the stages of wine-production. Mercier, ever at the showier end of this flamboyant commodity, takes visitors around its enormous cellars in a laser-controlled train, with some eye-catching special effects in the lift on the way down. Some of the smaller houses may give a rather more personal tour, but you should ask for an appointment first. After you have emerged, blinking, from the *caves*, a gentle ride through the vineyard villages (if you are in a fit state to drive!) makes an agreeable end to the outing. The most interesting and scenic wine routes are all signposted. Vines cloak the pale hillsides, each unnaturally pruned to give every bud the best possible chance of fruition. The labour-intensiveness of this operation is awesome. In the

more famous vineyards, each individual grape has a quantifiable value, so precious is this crop. If you arrive in winter you may well see stoves set out among the vines to ward off disastrous late frosts.

Stay or Eat:
Royal Champagne near Epernay (tel: 26 52 87 11); **Aux Armes de Champagne** at L'Epine near Châlons-sur-Marne (tel: 26 66 96 79); **Le Cheval Blanc** at Sept-Saulx (tel: 26 03 90 27).

Elegant Fontainebleau

♦♦♦
FONTAINEBLEAU
39 miles (63km) south
The massive and beautiful château is the main draw, but the great hunting forest that surrounds the town is a welcome retreat for all Parisian city-dwellers. It is an excellent place for picnics, walking, cycling and riding, but is very busy at weekends. The magnificent royal apartments of the château were transformed from medieval to Renaissance splendour by François I, and later kings also left their mark. The opulence of the décor is astonishing, especially the ceilings.

Stay or Eat:
L'Aigle Noir, 27 place Napoleon Bonaparte (tel: 64 22 32 65); there are plenty of less expensive places near the château.

♦
MEAUX
7 miles (11km) northeast
The closest town of historic interest to the Resort straddles the Marne upstream. The **Cathedral of St Etienne** is clearly visible as you drive towards the town, a Gothic structure with a lofty, light interior and a flamboyant 'Last Judgement' on the west door. Also in the old town are the **Old Chapter House** (a former tithe barn) and the 12th-century **Episcopal Palace**, now containing a **Fine Arts Museum**. The walled gardens are beautifully kept. Shaped like a bishop's mitre, they were originally laid out by André Le

EXCURSIONS FROM EURO DISNEY RESORT

Meaux brie, a local speciality

Nôtre, designer of the gardens at Versailles. In summer a well-attended *son et lumière* festival is usually held in the grounds of the palace.

Stay or Eat:
Hôtel de Richemont (no restaurant), quai de la Grande-Ile (tel: 60 25 12 10); **Auberge du Cheval Blanc**, 55 rue Victor-Clairet, Varreddes (tel: 64 33 18 03).

◆
MILLY-LA-FORET
48 miles (77km) southwest
Another attractive and rather less commercialised haunt, deep in Fontainebleau's extensive forest. Notable among its ancient buildings is a 15th-century **Market Hall**. The interior of the 12th-century **Chapel of St Blaise** was decorated by the poet-artist Jean Cocteau in 1959. The village has a reputation for medicinal herbs. About three miles (5km) northwards is the **Château de Courances**, built by Louis XIII and now open to the public.

◆◆
MORET-SUR-LOING
45 miles (72km) south
This picturesque place where the Impressionist artist, Alfred Sisley, spent the latter part of his life is a tranquil assembly of grey stone buildings reflected in the river, with an ancient bridge. The church of **Notre-Dame** is interesting outside and in: an unusual belltower and languid, elongated gargoyles decorate the exterior, while inside the chancel is ablaze with light from vivid, modern stained-glass windows. The half-timbered building nearby is an old hospital (notice the effigy of Saint James on one of the corner posts). **François I's House** (go through the archway of the town hall) has a fascinating gallery encrusted with Renaissance decorations (look for the salamander, symbol of François I).

Stay or Eat:
Auberge de la Terrasse, 40 rue de la Pêcherie (tel: 60 70 51 03); **Pavillon Bon Abri**, at Veneux-les-Sablons (3.5 km west), restaurant only (tel: 60 70 55 40).

◆◆
PROVINS
35 miles (56km) southeast
This hill town to the southeast of Marne-la-Vallée has a well-preserved upper town partly surrounded by medieval ramparts. The most striking feature is 12th-century **Caesar's Tower**, a turreted keep bristling with corner towers like stone warheads. **Place du Châtel** retains some very ancient houses. Also worth a look are the domed church of **St Quiriace**, with its plaque to Joan of Arc, the celebrated red roses brought back from Syria during the Crusades (legend has it that these found their way into the Lancastrian coat-of-arms), and some intriguing underground passages of dubious purpose, linking the upper and lower towns (guided tours available).

Stay or Eat:
Hostellerie Aux Vieux Remparts, 3 rue Couverte, Ville Haute (tel: 64 08 94 00).

◆◆◆
REIMS
68 miles (109km) northeast
This is a longish excursion, but a rapid and straightforward one along the A4. You will need some money for the tollgates if you use the motorway. After touring you can return on minor roads to Marne-la-Vallée. Reims is famous for two things: its magnificent cathedral, and its prominence as a centre for the champagne trade (see page 67), an honour it shares with the town of Epernay to the south. **Notre-Dame Cathedral** was for six centuries the coronation church of the kings of France. Despite numerous medieval fires and 20th-century wars, it still seems a fitting place for that role. The west front is glorious, especially at sunset. The graceful, pointed doorways lead the eye past countless sculpted kings to a giant rose window and the sturdy twin towers at either side. Look for the smiling angel on the left-

Tranquil Moret-sur-Loing

hand side. The interior, too, is smothered with sculpture, and these statues are rather better preserved. Inside, though, the eye is caught by the immense and elegant nave soaring to Gothic heights, the carved capitals (some with appropriately Bacchic scenes), and the wonderful stained glass (much has been restored after wartime damage, but it is still remarkable). Do not miss the Chagall window in the chapel behind the altar. When you emerge, walk round the back of the cathedral for a fine view of a forest of flying buttresses. Reims has several other buildings of note. The **Tau Palace**, next to the cathedral, houses ecclesiastical treasures and a series of 16th-century tapestries depicting the life of the Virgin. The **St Remi Basilica** is a successful mix of Gothic and Romanesque styles. There is a collection of medieval art and later tapestries housed in the abbey museum. The **Fine Arts Museum** in another ancient abbey (St Denis) contains a distinguished hoard of paintings from the 17th to 19th centuries (note the Corot landscapes). Two interesting mansions in the historic quarter are the **Hôtel de la Salle**, built in 1545, and the turreted **Hôtel Le Vergeur**, containing a local history museum. On a more contemporary note, the **French Automobile Museum** has collections of full-size and model vehicles.

Eat
Au Petit Comptoir, 17 rue Mars (tel: 26 40 58 58).

◆◆
VAUX-LE-VICOMTE, CHATEAU DE
28 miles (45km) south
Compared with Fontainebleau or Versailles, this château is small, but its moderate size seems only to enhance its attractiveness. It can more easily be appreciated and enjoyed in a single visit, while the pomp of the more grandiose châteaux is exhausting. The interior contains many charming features and fine antiques, but the grounds are most impressive: illusory vistas, neat topiary, canals and terraced parterres shift before the eye

Reims' magnificent Gothic cathedral

like an Escher painting as you walk among them.

The château has an interesting story. It was built by the ambitious politician Nicolas Fouquet, in 1656, and many famous artists have since woven their marks into its fabric. Le Vau was the architect, Le Nôtre designed its lovely gardens, and Le Brun supervised the interior. Fouquet was hungry for power and influence – his crest bore the emblem of a squirrel (the motto read, *How high shall I not climb*?). After his gorgeous château was completed in 1661, Fouquet made the disastrous mistake of inviting Louis XIV to dinner, to impress him. The king *was* impressed, so impressed that he seethed with jealousy and fury at this *parvenu*. Fouquet was arrested on a trumped-up charge and his possessions were seized by the king, who commissioned the very same artists to upstage Vaux-le-Vicomte with an even more ambitious project – Versailles. As Fouquet languished in perpetual imprisonment, he must have reflected many times that those who sup with autocratic monarchs need a long spoon.

Practical

This section (with the yellow band) includes food, drink, shopping, accommodation, nightlife, tight budget, special events, etc.

FOOD AND DRINK

This is a major element of the entertainment laid on at Euro Disney Resort, and it is a most unusual visitor who leaves without sampling any of it. To do so you would have to provide, carry and store your own supplies, or be prepared to travel some distance to find alternative eating places. There are no food shops or restaurants within walking distance of the Resort other than Disney ones, though picnic tables are provided near the Disneyland Hotel for those who bring their own food. (Remember, you are not allowed to take food or drinks into the Park.) In any case, eating Disney-style is all part of the experience, and the choice is extensive. Within the theme park there are many different restaurants, serving a great range of ethnic dishes, plus a range of *chariots gourmands* serving speciality foods, such as bagels and stir fry, and a number of carts selling popcorn, ice cream and beverages. In the Resort hotels

Flying high on Dumbo

and campground there are another 12 thematic restaurants (all open to any visitors, not just hotel residents, though it is always advisable to make a reservation before turning up). At Festival Disney, the entertainment complex just outside the gates of Euro Disneyland Park, there are another half-dozen restaurants, plus a dinner-show venue. Many, but not all Resort restaurants stay open all day. Wherever you are in the Park, you will find plenty of places to satisfy any sudden hunger pangs. Some restaurants have table service, at others you queue by counters, and some are no more than take-away snack bars. Child menus or child-size portions are served in table- or counter-service restaurants. Special diets, such as kosher, can also be catered for (with advance warning), as can group meals, birthday treats and business lunches. At peak times the restaurants within the theme park are geared to serve about 34,000 meals. Considering the speed and efficiency with which they do this, the quality is surprisingly high, and at least

FOOD AND DRINK

some notice is taken of many people's wish to eat healthier, less fat-laden diets. Overall, the range of food is very wide, though within each restaurant (particularly the counter-service ones), menu choices are kept reasonably limited for logistical reasons. Inevitably, however, 'fast food' abounds, prepared daily in mass-catering quantities. Where else in France, though, could you dine on a palm-fringed Caribbean shore with boats sliding past your table, or munch spare ribs in a high-raftered Wild West barn full of wagon wheels and hay rakes?

Eating at Euro Disneyland Park is not cheap, though some things are good value. If you are on a tight budget, avoid, or ration carefully, eating at the table-service restaurants. Stick to sensible, filling snacks from the *chariots gourmands*, such as baked potatoes in Frontierland, or beef and chicken kebabs in Adventureland. Any of the counter-service restaurants will provide you with a satisfying plateful of food without breaking the bank whenever you feel like a sit-down meal, and all table-service restaurants provide a three-course set meal for rather less than the *à la carte* price. You can pay for your meal in cash, and credit cards are accepted (but not by food carts). Guests staying in Resort hotels may use their Euro Disney charge cards at most places in the Park (although they are not accepted by food carts). The amount is then totalled on your credit card bill, which you pay as you check out.

Never a Drop to Drink

Euro Disneyland Park, like its cousins in Florida, California and Tokyo, is rigidly alcohol-free. No alcohol is served within its bounds, and none may be imported. The Park's priority 'guests' are children, and in such an environment adult pleasures (or vices) are thought to have no place. Walt's strict dictum prevails even in France, where children grow up accustomed to a watered glass

Tips

● Try to choose off-peak mealtimes to minimise queuing. Eat lunch before midday, or after 14.00hrs, and miss the 20.00–21.00hrs evening rush if you can. If you have already seen the parades, choose to eat when they are on. The restaurants are likely to be much emptier.

● At busy holiday times when the Park is crowded, you can make a same-day-only reservation at any table-service restaurant. The **Blue Lagoon Restaurant** (Adventureland) and **Auberge du Cendrillon** (Fantasyland) usually require booking at peak times. Do not worry if you cannot get into your first choice; there are plenty of other options. The last thing you need worry about here is starving!

● If the Park restaurants seem too busy, simply walk through the gates to Festival Disney, where you will have a choice of another half-dozen eating places, probably less busy at lunchtime.

of wine. So far, however, the iron Disney rule has not bent, and it shows no sign of doing so, despite much derision and amazement from the host country. It does seem slightly odd not to be able to have a glass of wine in a smart, expensive restaurant with an adult atmosphere like **Walt's – an American Restaurant**, for instance. For the time being, however, if you want a drink with your meal, you must leave the Park and head for Festival Disney, or any of the Resort hotels. Future theme parks, such as the proposed Disney MGM Studios – Europe, will serve alcohol in selected restaurants. But this Magic Kingdom stays teetotal.

All types of ice cream can be enjoyed

Eating in Euro Disneyland Park

Main Street, U.S.A.
Bagel cart You may spot this in Central Plaza, toasting bagels and adding toppings to all requirements. It is just one of many food carts (*chariots gourmands*) selling a variety of snacks and refreshments in the Park.
Cable Car Bake Shop Lots of wicked things most of us should not be eating are on offer in this agreeable (if dark) setting. There is booth seating, decorated with sepia photos of San Franciscan streetcars.
Casey's Corner Head here if you are a baseball freak. Hot dogs and chips are available. Eat them beside bats and balls and Coke logos, and beneath Tiffany lamps. You may be

FOOD AND DRINK

regaled with ragtime music.
The Coffee Grinder The coffee is fresh, but only one kind of coffee (plus espresso) is sold. Vintage coffee-making equipment is on display.
Cookie Kitchen A parting-shot temptation as you try to resist the Cable Car Bake Shop. This counter sells muffins and, of course, cookies (biscuits to Europeans).
The Gibson Girl Ice Cream Parlour Milkshakes, sundaes, banana splits and fruity ice-creams are all here in a pink–and–white candy-striped environment, with girls in frilly dresses and straw boaters.
The Ice Cream Company Just that, really.
Market House Deli An old-fashioned general store in the best Disney tradition. Sausages hang from the ceiling, and casks and lovely old tins deck the dresser shelves. There is also an ancient cast-iron stove and an old weighing machine. While admiring the décor, you can munch American sandwiches, such as hot pastrami on rye, and sample turkey and tuna salad.
Plaza Gardens Restaurant A spacious building with an outdoor patio, this is a good place to sit and watch the world, or the parades, go by. The sparkling 19th-century interior is full of columns, statues, stained-glass domes and mirrors. A wide choice of self-service fare consists of salads, hot dishes like Maryland crab cakes, and a luscious array of desserts (included in the price of a main course).

Explorers Club Restaurant serves exotic treats in Adventureland

Victoria's Home-Style Cooking Cosy domestic interiors from the 1890s set the tone for this counter-service. Eat Victoria's delicious 'pot pies' by the harmonium, or in the conservatory, perhaps watching a passing parade.

Walt's – an American Restaurant One of the smartest restaurants in the Park, this two-storey building offers elegant table service in nine intimate little dining-rooms, all on different themes. Lots of interesting items and paintings from Disney collections and archives. Seating inside, or on the outside patio. For good views of the parades, bag an (expensive) table upstairs near the window. Classy American food, including Veal Oscar, rack of lamb with goat's cheese, crab cakes and baked, stuffed Maine lobster. (A cheaper and simpler menu is offered downstairs and on the patio.)

Frontierland
Cowboy Cookout Barbecue A large barn houses this Wild-Western-style barbecue, with inside and outside seating for large numbers. The rustic theme includes agricultural implements, harnesses, quilts, wagon wheels, butter churns and so on, in a hay-loft/grain silo setting.

Fuente del Oro Restaurante Tex-Mex specials are all here: counter-service *tacos* and *fajitas*. The building is an attractive New Mexican one in adobe style, with a courtyard where you can eat and be regaled by the Mariachis, a Mexican group.

Last Chance Cafe Counter service for sandwiches, french fries and beverages. It is carefully styled as a bandit hideout.

The Lucky Nugget Saloon This houses a revue which is shown five times a day and is a counter-service restaurant. The menu features many favourite American dishes.

Silver Spur Steakhouse The smart folks of Thunder Mesa dine here, in stylish 19th-century surroundings, and (needless to say) prime rib steak is the speciality of the house.

Adventureland
Aux Epices Enchantées A counter-service restaurant in a Moorish building of red baked mud, decorated with ethnic animal ceramics, baskets and carvings. Lamb curry and Moroccan meatballs are staples, plus Mickey's fun meal (for children).

Blue Lagoon Restaurant This is located at the exit of Pirates of the Caribbean, and diners have a view of boats slipping past on their voyage of discovery. The scene is immediately attractive – a Caribbean night, lit by torches, with tropical vegetation all around – a delightful place to eat. Caribbean specialities and fish predominate: snapper, swordfish and other delicacies wrapped in banana leaves. As it is very popular, it is worth booking in advance if you want a table at a busy time.

Café de la Brousse A snack bar with thatched huts on a terrace overlooking Adventure

Isle, and a most pleasant place to sit. Sadly, the interesting-sounding North African specialities that were to be sold here, such as *kefta pitta* and yoghurt, have been replaced by hot dogs (albeit spicy ones) and chips, due to the patrons' lack of enthusiasm for anything exotic. Can this be gastronomic France?

Captain Hook's Galley
Sandwiches and cakes are available in this galleon anchored off Skull Rock, which is the haunt of pirates.

Explorers Club Restaurant
This has such an elaborate theme that it virtually constitutes an attraction in itself, but tucked away in the bamboo forest it makes a pleasant retreat. Built in colonial Victorian style, the club contains mementos of many exciting explorations: native masks, a plane propeller, safari gear, hunting trophies and photographs. You can choose to sit on the veranda, or inside – a central sunken dining area contains a great tropical tree where animated macaws and toucans perch; the Charter Room is a stone-built, cosier room with a fireplace.

Fantasyland
Au Chalet de la Marionnette Restaurant Fairytale frescos and Tyrolean charm smother this large counter-service restaurant. Chicken and chips and cheeseburgers, followed by apple strudel, are examples of the sort of fare it offers.

Auberge de Cendrillon
Cinderella's country inn is the smartest restaurant in Fantasyland, with beams and a

Inside Annette's Diner at Festival Disney

cosy fireplace. You will find Cinderella's pumpkin carriage in an alcove. Hosts and hostesses wear 17th-/18th-century costumes, in keeping with the elegant Louis XIV and XV furnishings. Try some European specialities: ham braised in cider, rack of lamb, or *coquilles St Jacques.*

Fantasia Gelati Italian ice-creams can be consumed outside on the patio.

March Hare Refreshments A wooden thatched cottage, serving beverages and un-birthday cakes. Bright tables are set outside for the tea party.

The Old Mill This old windmill will make the Dutch feel at home. Snacks, soft drinks and frozen yoghurt are on sale.

Pizzeria Bella Notte Italianate façades set the tone for a feast of pizza and pasta in a setting of hams and garlic. There is also a Bacchic theme of grapes and wine casks. Nothing, if you look carefully, is quite straight here.

Toad Hall Restaurant The expansive Mr Toad invites guests to partake of fish and chips wrapped in newspaper and roast beef sandwiches at his fine Elizabethan home. The interior is full of *Wind in the Willows* characters.

Discoveryland
Café des Visionnaires Next to Le Visionarium, this is another counter-service café decorated in bronze, copper, black and brown granite, and offering salads and stir fries; alfresco dining is offered, with covered

FOOD AND DRINK

Colourful signs promise sweet treats

verandas giving some protection from the elements. There are also wonderful views of the castle and shows.
Café Hyperion The Jules Verne airship, *Hyperion*, is suspended above the entrance to Videopolis. Inside, this fast counter-service restaurant offers salads, burgers and Italian fast food to carry to the auditorium for the show.
Chariots Gourmands A sausage cart (grilled sausages on bread with onions) and a donut cart produce the fastest food in Discoveryland.

Eating in Euro Disney Resort Accommodation

Camp Davy Crockett
An attractive log-cabin restaurant, **Crockett's Tavern** serves American home-style cooking for breakfast (and lunch in peak season) and dinner.

Disneyland Hotel
California Grill has an elegant open kitchen, where you can see Californian specialities being prepared. **Inventions** specialises in a blow-out buffet at a set price (and also hosts 'Character Breakfasts'). **Café Fantasia** is a pretty, cosy place with many Disney characters incorporated in its décor. This hotel is not the place to enjoy a simple snack at a reasonable price – go elsewhere, unless you can do justice to a full buffet-style breakfast or gourmet dinner.

Hotel Cheyenne
Guests eat at the **Chuckwagon Cafe**, a free-flow marketplace along Texan lines, where harnesses and bales of hay deck the high-raftered restaurant.

Hotel New York
Its restaurants are slick and smart, redolent of cocktails and dinner-dances and Big Band music. **Club Manhattan** offers a 1930s experience reminiscent of Harlem's 'Cotton Club', with fine dining in luxurious surroundings and dancing to bigband jazz. The **Club Manhattan Lounge** is the perfect venue for aperitifs or after-dinner drinks, while the **Parkside Diner** is also a good place to enjoy an evening drink

or a casual (but chic) meal.

Hotel Santa Fe

La Cantina is an imaginative Tex-Mex desert café, with petrol pumps and pick-up trucks among the food-stalls (an excellent place for breakfast).

Newport Bay Club

The **Yacht Club** is a speciality seafood restaurant, and from the **Cape Cod** restaurant guests overlook a flashing lighthouse by the shores of Lake Buena Vista, where 'Toobie' boats bob in summer.

Sequoia Lodge

Hearty grills and spit-roasts are available in the **Hunter's Grill**, while **Beaver Creek** is a good place for relaxing family meals. **Redwood Bar and Lounge** has a warm atmosphere.

Eating at Festival Disney

Several different sorts of American food can be eaten at the six restaurants here. **Annette's Diner** This is a 50s-style restaurant serving burgers and milkshakes amid period music (Elvis, Chuck Berry), while waitresses, on roller skates dash up and down aisles. Classic French and American automobiles provide interest outside.

Billy Bob's Country Western Saloon This Nashville saloon resounds with country-and-western music. Enjoy beer and chicken wings, or Mexican *nachos.*

Buffalo Bill's Wild West Show (See **Nightlife and Entertainment**, page 100).

Key West Seafood Shades of Florida Keys, a carefully styled dining area resembling an old bootlegger's hut overlooking the lake. If you eat by the Oyster Bar, lobsters gently twitch their claws and expire before the diners' gaze on great platefuls of seafood. Try Blue Crabs, two kinds of chowder or Key Lime Pie.

Los Angeles Bar & Grill Overlooking Lake Buena Vista, this two-storey restaurant and cocktail bar offers Californian specialities and pizza. Good selection of wines.

Sandwiches New York Style A New York deli, where giant pickle jars and elaborate speciality bread form the window display, and Broadway posters decorate the walls. Hot pastrami on rye, cream cheese on a bagel, or a classic bologna could precede Manhattan spice cake. You get substantial side dishes of potato salad or coleslaw.

Sports Bar Provides a non-stop round of televised sport on numerous TV monitors. TV dinners take the form of hot

Dance all evening at Billy Bob's Country Western Saloon

SHOPPING

dogs and sandwiches.

The Steakhouse Prime rib and T-bones are served in a building evoking a Chicago meat-packing warehouse. Classic wines (many Californian), and good desserts, such as brownies and cheesecakes, are sold.

Eating outside Euro Disney Resort

There are not many exciting restaurants close to Euro Disney Resort, but if you prefer a Gallic alternative to Disney fare and have a car, there are plenty of places worth trying within a 45-minute drive. Several of the older towns and villages have interesting restaurants (see **Excursions from Euro Disney Resort**, pages 66–75). Alternatively, of course, you can hop on the RER and head for central Paris. (For full details of places to eat in the capital, refer to *Essential Paris*.).

SHOPPING

'Merchandising' is all part of the entertainment at Euro Disney Resort, and you will find shops everywhere: in the hotels, at Festival Disney, and throughout the lands of the theme park. It is obviously a highly profitable operation for the Disney organisation, and the commercial tone may displease some visitors. But how much time and money you want to spend shopping is entirely up to you. There is no 'hard sell', no hassle or fleecing of the kind holidaymakers endure in many places. Just look if you like, and move on. It is a rare child, however, who will not take home at least one reminder of a trip to the Resort. Souvenirs come in all price ranges, from

Mickey Mouse appears on much Disney merchandise

wrapped candy-canes at F1.50 to enormous, hand-carved models of Mickey Mouse at around F65,000. You can even drive away in one of the classic automobiles at **Main Street Motors** if you are rich enough! They are all for sale.

Prices of goods at Euro Disney Resort are not low, but then neither is quality, even in items that are mass-produced and basically ephemeral. Whatever you feel about the aesthetics of mouse ears, at least they are not likely to disintegrate the second you walk out of the shop. Disney's rigorous standards apply to every item sold on its property, and that amounts to over 30,000 different pieces of merchandise from 26 different countries, in more than 50 shops. The shops in the Park are just as much an attraction as the rides.

Shops in Euro Disneyland Park

Main Street, U.S.A.
Boardwalk Candy Palace No children (and very few adults) get past this in a hurry. Here there are sweets and fudge, chocolates and toffees of all shapes and hues. Glass pillars, jars, and a Ferris Wheel are filled with a kaleidoscopic range. Almost behind the scenes the fudge-makers are hard at work. You can also buy saltwater taffy.

Disney & Co/Glass Fantasies
Yet more Disney souvenirs, in a yesteryear fairground setting. Mickey and Minnie wave from a hot-air balloon. Watch the man making cute little animals out of molten glass at Glass Fantasies.

Disney Clothiers, Ltd Fashion gear in a draper's shop, set in a private house of the period, with velvet curtains and a fireplace.

Disneyana Collectibles
Ceramics, jewellery boxes, lithographs, and the inked 'cels' from Disney animation pictures.

Emporium Mostly devoted to Disney souvenirs, this is the largest store in the Park. The old-fashioned pneumatic overhead cash transport system is fun to watch.

Harmony Barber Shop A splendid old-style barber's shop with a striped pole outside; inside among the tiles, mahogany and marble are badger-hair brushes and personal shaving mugs. You can have a real shave for F90 or a haircut for about F80, or you can just watch (anyone having a shave in Euro Disneyland Park is an exhibitionist). If you want something else to do, you can eavesdrop on a hand-crank telephone party line of 1910.

Harrington's Fine China & Porcelains The interior of crystal, stained glass and *faux* marble sets off a glittering array of glass and china. Some hand-painting takes place here.

Ribbons & Bows Hat Shop
Also on Town Square, this shop sells Victorian-style millinery and lots of other things to stick on your head, including hair slides, combs and mouse ears. You can also have a monogram embroidered by an old-fashioned sewing machine for free.

The Storybook Store On Town Square, this shop is designed

SHOPPING

for browsing. Disney film classics are retold in many languages – *Peter Pan*, *Alice in Wonderland* and so on. Also available are cassettes, novelty stationery, and Tigger, waiting to stamp your books with a Euro Disneyland Park memento if you like.

Town Square Photography
Film, video cassettes and other photographic equipment is sold here, in a setting of aged camera gear. There are also repair and express developing services and cameras and video cameras for hire. Silhouettes are cut in black paper by a silhouette artist.

Frontierland
Pueblo Trading Post
Interesting range of ethnic Mexican and Indian crafts: rugs, pottery, jewellery, dolls and the like. An adobe-style building surrounded by vegetation.
Thunder Mesa Mercantile Building A vast array of Wild West accoutrements, including jeans, coonskin caps, stetsons, cowboy boots, and so on is available at this log cabin. Also Wild-Western-style provisions.
Woodcarver's Workshop This small stall specialises in wooden animals, but you can also have your name carved, if you like.

Adventureland
Adventureland Bazar One of the Park's most exciting shopping experiences. Its oriental-looking onion domes are the land's most obvious landmark from Central Plaza. Inside is a maze of thick stone walls and passageways, recreating the world of the Thousand and One Nights. In its winding alleys and courtyards you will find traders and artisans at work beating copper or making jewellery amid piles of rugs, baskets and leather. The five individual shops are given exotic names: Les Trésors de Schéhérazade, La Reine des Serpents, L'Echoppe d'Aladin, Le Chant des Tam-Tams, La Girafe Curieuse. They sell goods from many countries: brass bells, Egyptian perfume bottles, sandalwood boxes from Morocco and African pottery and carvings.

Le Coffre du Capitaine Pirate gear is on sale in this shop at the exit of Pirates of the Caribbean: pieces-of-eight, cutlasses, eye-patches, skull-and-crossbone hats and flags.
Trader Sam's Jungle Boutique A tantalising collection of odd souvenirs from interesting parts of the globe: a stuffed alligator and an old canoe decorate his palm-thatched hut. Jewellery, shells and the necessities of exploration, such as a watch incorporating a compass.

Fantasyland
La Bottega di Geppetto (Geppetto's Workshop.) More unusual toys: music boxes, cuckoo clocks, puzzles, marionettes and the like.
La Boutique du Château Within the castle, this festive shop is a year-round hoard of decorations and ornaments.
Le Brave Petit Tailleur Mickey Mouse takes up the role of the medieval tailor in this clothes shop selling Disney character garments.
La Chaumière des Sept Nains

More Disney apparel and stuffed toys, in the cottage of the Seven Dwarfs.

La Confiserie des Trois Fées Edible goodies can be found here, in the forest cottage of the three good fairies from *Sleeping Beauty*.

La Ménagerie du Royaume Animals rule, OK: carousel horses, and all kinds of creatures, including Disney ones.

Merlin l'Enchanteur Within the castle, this shop is hard to resist. Designed as the magician's workshop, the walls are full of intriguing inventions and glittering toys: kaleidoscopes, jewellery, figurines, chess sets and even a jewelled crown.

Sir Mickey's Mickey Mouse is shown fighting with a giant beanstalk here. Disney souvenirs are sold inside.

Discoveryland

Constellations Souvenirs for explorers, hi-tech toys and Disney clothes in a startling room rather like a planetarium.

Seven Dwarfs for sale

An alchemist's still and other scientific instruments decorate the shop. Leonardo's *Ornithopter* flying machine hangs from the ceiling, with Mickey Mouse at the controls.

Star Traders All kinds of space-age gadgets and games can be found in this octagonal building: hologram badges, magnets, puzzles and so forth.

Shops in Euro Disney Resort

The Hotels

Each of the hotel shops, besides stocking a range of staples, features a few special items appropriate to its theme. So Hotel Cheyenne's shop sells Wild West gear and toy guns, and the Hotel Santa Fe's shop stocks cactus mugs. Do not bother to shop around within the Resort; prices are identical for the same items everywhere. Images of Mickey Mouse are endlessly reproduced on all manner of artefacts: soft toys, mugs, pencils, T-shirts, candies and novelties of all kinds, including a peculiarly French craze for ornamental pins. All the hotel shops have significant

store space given to Disney goods.

Festival Disney
The Disney Store has a collection of transport – trains, planes, cars – amid a vast range of 'character merchandise', as it is called in Disneyspeak. Here, Mickey Mouse reigns supreme. **Team Mickey** sells Mickey Mouse sportswear, and **Hollywood**

Adventureland Bazar

Pictures has movie souvenirs (posters, books, photographs, and so on), many from The Walt Disney Studios. Racks of T-shirts and casual leisurewear deck many a shop. More out of the ordinary is Festival Disney's **Buffalo Trading Company**. If you want to 'shop American style', do not miss the **Streets of America Shop**. For beachwear, head for the **Surf Shop**. The **Post Office** is located in Festival Disney, although stamps can also be bought at hotels.

Tips
• Beware of spending too much time in the shops. You will regret not going on the rides if you run out of time, and there are plenty of shops outside the Park to browse in at leisure.
• If you want to do some shopping, do not leave things to the last minute, when you will find that the queues are long. Shop in the early or mid-afternoon, when you feel like a break. You can always leave bulky things in the lockers beneath Main Street Station.
• The 'user-friendly' Disney shops may seem a kleptomaniac's paradise. Most of the items on display can be handled. Security is very, very low key (in fact, completely invisible), but it certainly exists and 'appropriate measures' are taken if necessary.
• Besides cash (French francs), you can pay for items in Disney stores by traveller's cheque, Eurocheque or credit card (American Express, Visa, Diner's Club or Access/Mastercard only). Personal cheques may only be drawn in French banks, and you will need ID. If you are staying in a Resort hotel, you can use your Disney card to charge purchases directly to your credit card account, payable when you check out. Currency exchange offices are also available in Adventureland and Fantasyland.
• If by any chance something you buy is faulty, take it back to the shop with your receipt and it will be exchanged. If you have left the Park, send the item, with a photocopy of the receipt and a letter explaining the defect to the manager of the store where you bought it. Write to him or her c/o Euro Disney SCA, BP 100, F-77777 Marne-la-Vallée, CEDEX 4, France. You will then receive a refund.

ACCOMMODATION

Visitors can choose to stay at one of the six Disney Resort hotels, or at the campground. If you choose either, you will be able to enjoy certain privileges denied to off-site visitors, such as guaranteed access to the theme park (which may close to other visitors on severely crowded days). The hotels themselves are imaginatively designed and very comfortable, each a separate mini-theme park in itself – Manhattan or New Mexican, New English or Wild Western. If you want a total Disney experience, you should stay at the Resort. All the hotels are within walking distance of the entrance gates to Euro Disneyland Park, though to make life even easier a fleet of buses whirls round the Resort at frequent intervals, taking visitors to the bus station, less than five minutes' walk from the turnstiles. Although the campground is several kilometres away, it is connected to the Park by a regular and efficient bus service.

You can choose to stay at a hotel or motel outside the Resort, but there are no off-site hotels and motels within walking distance. If you have notions of staying in some quaint country *auberge* within a few minutes' drive of the Resort, dispel them now. Most types of accommodation that serve the Euro Disney Resort area of Marne-la-Vallée are modern and purely functional, consisting of box-like motels or business hotels. One or two of the older hotels in neighbouring villages have anticipated increased demand by adding new bedroom blocks, often in rather a characterless style.

If you are touring the area by car, and fancy a day or two at the Euro Disneyland Park (but do not regard the Disney experience as of paramount importance), you might choose to stay further afield in a place of historic interest, such as Meaux or Fontainebleau, or even perhaps in the Champagne country to the east. You should be prepared for a drive of 1 hour or more to reach the Resort.

Last but not least, you can opt to stay in Paris and travel each day to Euro Disney Resort by public transport. Many tour operators also offer inclusive deals using French or Euro Disney hotels at all price levels.

Euro Disney Resort Hotels

All six Euro Disney Resort hotels lie quite close together just outside the gates of the Park, around the artificial stretches of water christened **Lake Buena Vista** and **Rio Grande**. Hotels are classified in four categories: luxury, first class, moderate and economy. The more expensive ones are closer to the Park entrance gates. Each hotel is very different in appearance, but all are highly theatrical, endeavouring to give their guests a variety of thematic experiences. The hotel architecture is a subject in itself. Several world-renowned architects have created the hotels, and the ways in which themes have been

Disneyland Hotel

encapsulated are startling and innovative. If you are interested in architecture you may wish to obtain a *Connaissance des Arts* publication about Euro Disney Resort (available in French and English in some of the shops), which contains verbatim interviews with the architects and explains their ideas, with excellent photographs.

All of the Resort hotels have high standards of comfort and cleanliness, and aim to provide the level of service appropriate to any Disney facility. When the Resort first opened, however, staffing levels seemed inadequate to cope with queues at reception areas, and some waiting times were unacceptably long. The more expensive hotels have more elaborate trappings than the economy ones, but all of them have some non-smoking rooms, and some are suitable for the disabled. All except the Hotel Santa Fe and Hotel Cheyenne have swimming pools and health clubs. Note that there is no porter service at the moderate or economy hotels, or at the campground, and no trolleys are provided to help wheel luggage, so travel light! These complexes are large and spread out.

As some hotels may open on a seasonal basis, and hotel rates fluctuate according to season, check all reservation details first with your travel agent or with Euro Disney Resort Central Reservations (see the **Directory** on page 121 for address and telephone numbers).

Disneyland Hotel
(Luxury – 500 rooms)
This rambling pink confection is one of the most striking landmarks of Euro Disney Resort. In terms of bedrooms it is the smallest of the hotels, though you would never think so to look at it. Its florid, Victorian-style gables and turrets, topped with pointed

ACCOMMODATION

Newport Bay Club

are a huge reception lobby, whose chandelier drips with ivy leaves, and a promenade, where a piano is played in an elegant lounge. The three restaurants offer a variety of lavish fare. This is the most expensive hotel in the Resort, with many luxury facilities. Finding your way around its complex blocks, though, takes some time.

Hotel New York

(First Class – 574 rooms)
If you have seen Florida's Walt Disney World Resort you will instantly recognise the post-modernist handiwork of the celebrated American architect Michael Graves. His fantasy hotels in Orlando have a similarly extravagant style. Hotel New York recreates the landscapes of the Big Apple (minus those unforgettable exterior fire escapes) in a subtle palette of warm terracotta, dove grey and soft salmon. Inside, every last feature of the hotel, down to the Empire State Building lampstands in the bedrooms, echoes the theme. The effect is sophisticated, but fun. It is a more adult environment than the Disneyland Hotel, and this hotel hosts Disney's lucrative sideline, the convention business (a very large conference centre is attached, providing the most extensive meeting-room facilities in the Paris area). Rooms overlook paved plazas or shady gardens and tennis courts. Though first class, Hotel New York is slightly less expensive than the Disneyland Hotel. Both offer

white finials, triumphantly straddle the entrance gates to the Park. From Main Street, just inside the turnstiles, it is as noticeable a fantasy feature as the castle, and many rooms have views of the Park. The hotel seems utterly confident of its status as the flagship, and it is easily the most Disneyesque of all the strange buildings in the Resort area. Designed by the architects of Disney 'Imagineering', it evokes the grand seaside palaces that graced the smart resorts of Florida and California at the turn of the century. It is very much a family hotel, with thematic references to Disney cartoon characters. A giant Mickey Mouse clock on the central façade shows guests the time. The hotel's main features

Castle Club VIP service with luxurious suites, a private lounge and additional privileges for an extra charge. (There is no Castle Club VIP Service at Hotel New York in winter).

Newport Bay Club

(Moderate – 1,098 rooms)
The irregular, creamy clapboard architecture with the grey-green roofs conjures up a tang of salt spray and a whiff of ozone. This is New England, the Atlantic seaboard. The New York architect Robert Stern designed this elaborate whimsy with classical touches, reminiscent of the Yacht and Beach Clubs at Walt Disney World Resort in Florida. Inside, the atmosphere is elegantly restful in shades of blue and grey. Bedrooms and corridors continue the nautical theme, with porthole windows and ship's tiller headboards. The **Fisherman's Wharf** bar-lounge is relaxing to sit in.

Sequoia Lodge

(Moderate – 1,011 rooms)
Embryonic redwood forests surround the timber wings and shallow, copper-green rooftops of this hotel, bent on recreating the atmosphere of an American National Park lodge. Décor consists of lots of redwood veneer and grey stone. The main feature of the bar area is a huge, stone-faced fireplace, where there are real log fires. The imaginative swimming pool has waterslides and hot springs, and is one of this hotel's most attractive points. Bedrooms are decorated with wooden furniture and patchwork quilts.

Hotel Cheyenne

(Economy – 1,000 rooms)
A taste of the Old Wild West. Here you will find a life-size stage set of *High Noon*, where covered wagons stand in the streets, and you check in at the Town Bank by the Hangman's Tree. You could be sleeping in any one of 14 separate, wood-framed buildings. The **Red Garter Saloon** is the place for a drink, but do not expect a peaceful time here. It is very much geared to families, and the atmosphere is cheerfully gregarious. In the bedrooms, Western fans will be delighted to find stetson hat mirrors and bucking broncos on the walls, while **Fort Apache**, in the grounds, is a new style of adventure playground.

Hotel Santa Fe

(Economy – 1,000 rooms)
We are somewhere in New Mexico at this hotel, marked by a large 'drive-in cinema screen' sign bearing the likeness of Clint Eastwood. A complex of blocks encapsulating the atmosphere of the desert lies behind it, with colours ranging from blues and violets to earth tones. Between the blocks are mysterious sculpted objects, a flying saucer, a volcano, rusting automobiles and giant cacti. The theories behind the architecture of this hotel are complex, and it is worth following the various 'trails' between the buildings that architect Antoine Predock created (the Trail of Legends, the Trail of Infinite Space, and so on). Bedrooms are tastefully designed, using Pueblo Indian themes. Of the two economy

ACCOMMODATION

hotels, the Hotel Santa Fe costs slightly less.

Camp Davy Crockett

(414 cabins, 181 campsites)
The campground is some way from the theme park, south of the A4 beyond the golf course, so be prepared to rely on the bus service if you do not bring your own car. An extensive 138-acre (56-ha) patch of mature oak and beech woodland allows visitors to sample an outdoor experience in pioneer style. By staying in one of the luxurious trailer-home cabins, you can do so in great comfort. There is a microwave oven, telephone, toaster, dishwasher, maid service (every other day), and a large colour TV. If you prefer, you can bring your own tent or caravan and set up camp in the trees, cooking baked beans over a primus stove or taking advantage of Crockett's Tavern. Each site is supplied with water, toilets and electricity, as well as a barbecue and picnic table. Other features include a small farm of domestic animals, sports facilities (tennis, volleyball, basketball, *pétanque*), and a beautiful and cleverly landscaped swimming pool with waterfalls, bridges, whirlpools, slides and water cannon, housed in a huge, light and airy log cabin. Buses pick up passengers regularly from three points in the campground for the theme park; bicycles or electric golf carts can be hired to ride round the site. An on-site shop provides a wide range of groceries and toiletries, films, sweets and toys.

Off-site Accommodation

Numerous box-like motels are springing up around Marne-la-Vallée to cater for the new influx of visitors. Many of these belong to chains such as Campanile, Primavere, Mercure, Altea, Fimotel, Climat, Ibis, Novotel or Formule 1, providing 1- to 3-star accommodation. Do not expect anything very fancy or interesting; these are purely intended to provide practical, adequate accommodation for brief stop-overs. Many are in charmless locations on busy roads and suffer from traffic noise; a few are handily placed for the RER stations on the Marne-la-Vallée line, but for most you need a car. The newer ones have better facilities (good bathrooms, telephones and so on), and are generally more smartly decorated than the older ones. Most provide some sort of restaurant, where the food, if not exactly *haute cuisine*, is authentically French and less expensive than in Euro Disney Resort. Many establishments work with tour operators, and you will find them listed in brochures offering Euro Disney Resort packages. Most of the big chains produce brochures, with useful location plans. If you prefer small, privately run family hotels, get the local *Logis de France* list. The Ile-de-France Maison du Tourisme (at Festival Disney) produces a useful list of local accommodation and is very helpful about where to stay. It will make reservations for a small fee.

Suggested Off-Site Hotels

Two good, brand-new hotels near Euro Disney Resort are modelled closely on American motel chains: the **Days Hotel** at 15 avenue du Golf, 77600 Bussy St Georges (tel: 64 66 30 30), and the **Comfort Inn** at rue de la Ferme du Pavillon, 77400 Chanteloup-en-Brie (tel: 64 30 00 00). Less expensive, independent small hotels with slightly more character include **Acostel**, 336 avenue de la Victoire (R.N.3), 66100, Meaux (tel: 64 33 28 58); **Bacchus**, 9 place des Tilleuls, 77450 Trilbardou (tel: 60 01 90 55); **L'Auberge Fleurie**, 3 rue St Denis, 77174 Villeneuve St Denis, 77174 Villeneuve St Denis (tel: 60 25 01 00); and **Hôtel du Centre**, 2 rue Juies-Herret, 77144 Montevrain (tel: 64 30 25 14). Two more expensive and luxurious places, with peaceful settings

Resort hotels offer high standards of comfort

and more ambitious facilities slightly further from the Resort, are **Le Manoir** at Départementale 402, 77610 Fontenay-Tresigny, a country house set in parkland (tel: 64 25 91 17), and **La Louveterie**, 10 route des Faremoutiers, 77515 St Augustin , a quiet, stylish restaurant with rooms (tel: 64 03 37 59).

Staying Further Afield

The countryside immediately around Euro Disney Resort is of little interest from the tourist's point of view, but within a couple of hours' drive are a number of places with good hotels, well worth a visit. (See **Excursions from Euro Disney Resort** on pages 66–75) .

ACCOMMODATION

Staying in Paris

There is little point in choosing to stay in one of Paris's nondescript easterly suburbs, thinking you will be that much nearer the Park. You will miss out on both the bright lights of Euro Disney Resort and the bright lights of Paris. You may not even save travelling time; many RER trains skip stations between Vincennes and Marne-la-Vallée, so the service from outer suburbs can be less frequent than from the centre. There is obviously a vast number of hotels to choose from in Paris, and you will see these listed in tour operators' brochures at all price levels and in all areas. If you are booking independently, one of the best areas to choose is the Marais district, where the Pompidou Centre and Hôtel de Ville lie north of Notre Dame. There are three reasons for this: first, it is one of the most interesting and charming areas of old Paris; second, it has a number of small, good-value hotels of real character; and third, it is on RER line A4 to Euro Disney Resort, taking about 40 minutes from Châtelet–les–Halles or the Gare de Lyon (see the **Directory** on pages 113–14, for more about transport).

Suggested Parisian Hotels

Hôtel des Celestins, 1 rue Charles V (tel: 48 87 87 04); **Hôtel de la Bretonnerie**, 22 rue Ste-Croix-de-la-Bretonnerie (tel: 48 87 77 63); **Hôtel St Merry**, 78 rue de la Verrerie (tel: 42 78 14 15); **Hôtel du Vieux Marais**, 8 rue du Plâtre (tel: 42 78 47 22); **Hôtel de la Place des Vosges**, 12 rue de Birague (tel: 42 72 60 46); **Hôtel Axial Beaubourg**, 11 rue du Temple (tel: 42 72 72 22); **Hôtel St Louis**, 75 rue St-Louis-en-l'Ile (tel: 46 34 04 80).

Packages

The standard price of a Euro Disney Resort hotel ranges from about £55 to nearly £200 per room per night in high season (1992 rates), though it is worth remembering that all Resort hotel bedrooms take four people. However, inclusive Euro Disney packages offer savings on two- or three-night stays, but these must be booked five days in advance through Disney's Central Reservation Office. If you book a package at a Resort hotel, or at the campground (cabins only, not tents), you get unlimited entry to the Park during your stay, as well as use of local transport, welcome cocktails and so on (you make your own way to Euro Disney Resort). Contact Euro Disney SCA, BP 105, Central Reservations, F-77777 Marne-la-Vallée, CEDEX 4, France, for

Euro Disneyland Park excels at parades

further details, including the Euro Disney brochure, *Guide to Magic Holidays*. (See also page 121.) Many tour operators offer package deals which include travel to the Resort and Park entrance fees. You stay either at Euro Disney Resort hotels, or at off-site motels nearby, or at hotels in Paris. Few, however, can produce a much cheaper deal than you could put together by yourself (P&O European Ferries gives notably good value). What you buy with a package holiday is the convenience of having all arrangements made for you, by agents with more influence than an independent traveller. If you decide to book a package holiday, look first at Euro Disney Resort 'preferred travel partners' (British Airways and P&O European Ferries), and at the Resort's six 'selected operators': Paris Travel Service, Cresta, Wallace Arnold, Sunworld, Airtours and Eurocamp. All these operators offer package holidays at Euro Disney Resort hotels and have a privileged relationship with the Disney organisation, entitling clients to certain priority treatment. Prices, even among these operators, vary widely for substantially the same package. A great many other operators offer packages, many of them using much cheaper accommodation off site. Take care to read the small print about what your package actually includes, and check how much time you will have at the Park. Beware of some cheap coach tours which exclude Park admission costs, or the cost of transfer to hotels.

NIGHTLIFE AND ENTERTAINMENT

While the Park is open, Euro Disney Resort is one long round of entertainment. Besides all the individual attractions, there is always something extra going on somewhere. As you arrive you are greeted by smartly dressed marching bands or instrumentalists like the **Keystone Kops**. In the different lands of the Park, you will find other musicians: an African steel band, the **Tams-Tams Africains** here, or the Mexican **Mariachis** there. Impromptu scenes may surprise you: for instance, a sudden shoot-out on the rooftops of **The Lucky Nugget Saloon**. In Frontierland there is a chance of running into the **card-sharp** doing his version of Find the Lady (he is not allowed to take money from anyone), and there is **Dr Livingstone**, I presume, playing the ukelele and telling extraordinary tales in Adventureland. Not all these entertainers are in the Park every day. Ask at **City Hall** if you want to see anything in particular.

Regular Shows in Euro Disneyland Park

Performances take place several times a day, at **Le Théâtre du Château**, **Videopolis**, or **Fantasy Festival Stage**. As you go into the Park, be sure to pick up an *Entertainment Program* listing show times. The programme rotates weekly, and most shows last about 20 minutes. The **Fantasy Festival Stage** hosts performances of music and

NIGHTLIFE AND ENTERTAINMENT

Buffalo Bill's Wild West Show

and heads for Paris, where she encounters Pierre Paradis, the man of her dreams, and collects a dance troupe. **Buffalo Bill's Wild West Show** is more expensive, involving stunt riding, lasso tricks and some bewildered buffalo. It is an enthusiastically presented show featuring 'Annie Oakley' (the best of the riders), and assorted cowboys and Indians. Based on the touring Wild West Show which wowed France in 1889 during the Exposition Universelle, the theme continues to fascinate its European audience. Apparently even Queen Victoria was amused by the original! Western-style spare ribs and chili accompany the show. There are also lots of silly games, in which the audience is invited to participate, and of course the kid wins the shooting match!

dancing in its 500-seat auditorium. You can sit out of the rain for this one, under the roof of Fantasyland Station. Five times a day **Rock Shock**, a rock 'n' roll video in 3-D, with music by David Hallyday, takes place. The show lasts about 20 minutes.

Parades and Fireworks
For full details of these, refer to the **What to See** section on pages 38–40.

Dinner Shows
At present there are two dinner shows, one in the theme park's Frontierland (at **The Lucky Nugget Saloon**), the other at **Festival Disney**. **The Lucky Nugget Saloon**, all gilded lights and tasselled curtains, is horseshoe-shaped like a theatre, and puts on five 30-minute shows a day. The plot is a corny but enjoyable tale of a fun-loving gal who strikes it rich

Festival Disney
When the Park closes early, there are still things to do. In Festival Disney, just beyond the Disneyland Hotel, there are night clubs and bars, shops and restaurants that all stay open late. **Hurricanes** is the venue for dancing, with 'high-energy' lighting and music, snazzy cocktails and sunset parties on the veranda. Here there are no less than 20 different video screens to entertain you, plus four separate bars to choose between. **Billy Bob's Country Western Saloon** has a five-piece cowboy band and a Texan atmosphere. Pool tables provide additional entertainment. (See above for **Buffalo Bill's Wild West Show**.)

Hotel Entertainment

All of the Euro Disney hotels provide some sort of live music. Hotel New York's **Club Manhattan** restaurant has live jazz reminiscent of the Cotton Club. The **Disneyland Hotel** lounge is more Victorian in style, with entertainers in period costume. Impromptu happenings may occur in fine weather at **Hotel Cheyenne** or at **Camp Davy Crockett**.

Outside Euro Disney Resort

Among the bright lights of Paris any number of high- or low-brow entertainments or restaurants await visitors, from the fleshpots of Pigalle and the Moulin Rouge to the Opéra, or Left-Bank café-theatre. The tourist office in Festival Disney will give you lots of advice. Get one of the 'What's On' magazines, such as *L'Officiel des Spectacles* or *Pariscope* (out each Wednesday) for full listings. On Thursdays the Musée d'Orsay, one of Paris's most enjoyable museums, stays open late; and on Mondays or Wednesdays you can visit sections of the Louvre until 22.00hrs. Paris looks especially nice at night from the top of the Eiffel Tower (open till 23.00hrs), and the Bateaux Mouches run during the evenings, too. Remember to check the time of your last train (usually at about 00.30hrs) back to Marne-la-Vallée!

Not to be outshone in the contest for tourist revenue are several historic towns near Euro Disney Resort. They put on *son et lumière* shows and other events during the summer (Meaux, Fontainebleau and Chantilly). And you can also visit Vaux-le-Vicomte by candlelight on some summer Saturdays.

Main Street at night

WEATHER AND WHEN TO GO

When the Park was first planned, there was some debate over Disney's prudence in placing it in cool Northern France, instead of in Spain or somewhere near the Mediterranean. There is no doubt that climate will play a significant role in the future success of Euro Disney Resort, perhaps more than anyone would have imagined. Keen Disney fans who remember the sunshine of Florida or California may be dismayed to find chilly European drizzle and cloud. The facts are incontrovertible: the Resort looks truly magical in the sun, when its colours sparkle and the gilded finials of the castle

The Cheshire Cat points the way in Alice's Curious Labyrinth

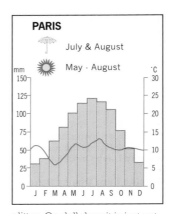

glitter. On dull days it is just not the same. If you have any choice in the matter, try to visit on a fine day. But do not abandon the idea of going simply because the weather is poor. For one thing, the Park is almost certain to be less crowded, and you will see far more attractions. Disney 'Imagineers' have considered the weather, of course, and have made a number of modifications to the design of the Park to suit Northern France's climate. All visitor areas have central heating and air conditioning, and in many places, particularly in hotels, shops and restaurants, you will find cheerful log fires roaring away in great chimneys. More of the attractions and queuing areas are covered over than in Disney parks in America, and most hotel swimming pools are covered. Large eaves also extend over queuing areas to protect waiting crowds at the attractions.

Marne-la-Vallée's climate, described as 'temperate' in

Disney's promotional literature, is actually rather dryer than that of coastal France. The wettest months are from November to January and from March to May (all have more than 15 days of rainfall – not necessarily, of course, all day long). Highest temperatures are predictably in July and August, when a sunhat is definitely advisable. Between May and June and September and October there are pleasantly equable temperatures, and daytime highs are between 16 and 21°C (61 and 70°F). Otherwise, it is unusual to experience climatic extremes or sharp seasonal variations. Average temperatures stay above freezing all year round, and it rarely gets too hot to stay outdoors during the middle of the day.

If you have children you may be tied to school holiday times, but to avoid crowds, try to miss popular French holidays, such as Labour Day (Fête du Travail, 1 May), Victory Day (Fête de la Libération, 8 May), Bastille Day (Fête Nationale, 14 July), Assumption (Assomption, 15 August), Hallowe'en/All Saints' (Toussaint, 31 October–1 November), and, of course, Christmas and New Year. You can also expect more crowds around Easter and Whitsuntide. French school holidays are staggered, lasting over several weeks (mid-April to mid-May; early July to early September). August is a traditional holiday month for many Parisians, and those who have not headed for the south coast may well visit the Park then.

HOW TO BE A LOCAL

Though France is the host country of Euro Disney Resort, both staff ('cast members', as they are known in the Resort), and visitors ('guests') are a great mix of nationalities. French and English are the official languages, and you will find notices, show scripts and so on in both. Many of the staff speak one or more other languages, particularly German, Dutch, Spanish or Italian. They are young and easy-going, including many students doing a Disney season. Many of the cast members in the Park and at the hotels are Dutch, chosen for their formidable linguistic skills and their calm, unflappable temperaments. You will obviously find many French staff, too. Their communication skills are impressive, but not always completely fluent. It is always appreciated if you are prepared to meet your hosts halfway with language. If you have a little French, why not practise it here in this helpful and friendly environment? After all, you will probably need to use it if you have any plans to visit Paris or tour the region afterwards.

Apart from language, the mood is American, and the rigorous Disney discipline is imposed, as in US Disney parks. Everyone is neat and tidy, everyone smiles, and everyone wishes you a nice day. Many of the European cast and guests are still getting used to the Disney aproach. Remember to smile a lot. And have a nice day!

Everything in the Park is geared to children

CHILDREN

Children of all ages visit Euro Disney Resort; anyone aged 12 or over counts as an adult and must pay the full entrance price. Children under three can enter free. Pricing policies put quite a lot of pressure on families to make the most of every minute they have in the theme park. Unfortunately, children are not always easily programmable. They have a disconcerting habit of not being in the mood for theme-parking on the days you have tickets. Build in some time off, such as a break in the middle of the day, or even a sleep at the hotel. The main thing is to prevent them from becoming overtired. And if the weather is hot, make sure they get enough to drink and are protected from the sun.

The parades and shows, and appearances by Disney characters in costume, are things most children seem to love. Make sure you have some film in your camera when Mickey Mouse turns up, or you will never be forgiven. You can find **Disney characters** in the Park every day, or in the hotels at 'Character Breakfasts'. For some *real* animals, head for the farms at **Critter Corral** and **Frontierland**, or visit **Camp Davy Crockett**, where there are ponies to ride in the spring and summer seasons. The electronic **games rooms** and **arcades** in all of the hotels are expensive, but ever-popular with today's hi-tech child.

No two children react in quite the same way to Euro Disneyland Park's attractions. Most take them in a matter-of-fact way, and some are completely blasé. Others get wildly excited, a few frightened or sick. It is quite difficult to assess what may alarm a child. Very young ones may find the spooks in **Phantom Manor**, the eerier sections of **Pirates of the Caribbean**, or the Wicked Queen in **Blanche-Neige et les Sept Nains** (Snow White and the Seven Dwarfs) quite perturbing. For further information on attractions for young or older children, and for contra-indications, see **Planning Your Visit** on pages 28–32.)

Facilities

Child facilities are well publicised throughout the Park. There is a **Baby Care Center** near Plaza Gardens Restaurant (at the end of Main Street) where nappies can be changed, bottles warmed and basic necessities purchased. Pushchairs (strollers) can be rented for use within the Park at **Town Square Terrace** near the main entrance. There are no

Balloons are always popular with children

restrictions on pushchairs being brought into the Park. Lost children will be shepherded to the **Lost Children Office** and looked after until you find them - ask any cast member for advice. You can leave children supervised by cast members at the **Neverland Club** children's theater in **Festival Disney**. Here there is a games room with a Peter Pan theme, where children from three to ten years are entertained and supervised for up to five hours. (Open from 17.00hrs until late evening.) All of the Euro Disney hotels can provide baby-sitting services.

TIGHT BUDGET

Taking a family to Euro Disney Resort is by no means a budget holiday option. But there are ways to cut some of the costs, and if you maximise the use of your time at the Park, it is unlikely that you will feel you have had a poor deal. There is, after all, an enormous amount to do, and if you compare the attractions of Euro Disneyland Park with other forms of family entertainment (other theme parks, for example, or some museums in central Paris) the inclusive entrance charges begin to look pretty reasonable for such a lot of fun (over 15 hours a day in high season, if you have the stamina).

● Extras can mount up if you are not careful – all the ice creams and soft drinks, the T-shirts and mouse ears. A few of these are part of the experience, but with children in tow you may have to restrain some impulse buys.

● If you have children, or do not mind sharing a bedroom with friends, you can save money by staying in just one room at **Hotels Cheyenne** or **Santa Fe**, or at **Camp Davy Crockett.** Most Disney hotel bedrooms can accommodate families of four; trailer cabins take up to six people. If there are just two of you, it will be cheaper to stay in a local motel or small hotel near, but not actually in, the Resort. But bear transport in mind – you may need a car. If you are relying on public transport, choose an

inexpensive hotel somewhere near a convenient metro or RER station in central Paris (preferably on or with easy connections to line A4, the Marne-la-Vallée–Chessy line).

• Choose counter-service cafés or *chariots gourmands* for snacks, rather than more expensive table-service restaurants. If you are feeling very economical, you do not have to buy any food at all. You can bring your own, and eat it in the picnic area *outside* the Park. You cannot bring any food or drink through the turnstiles. Leave your hamper either in your car, or with Guest Storage near the entrance to the Park.

Fantasyland's Mad Hatter's Tea Cups ride

• Try to assess realistically how many days you want to spend at the Resort. There is enough at the theme park to keep most people happy for two days, three if you want to revisit some of the attractions. You can save money by buying a two- or three-day passport (best value is the three-day one, which reduces the adult daily entrance charge by about 20 per cent). You do not have to use it on consecutive days.

• Take some light raingear with you if the weather looks doubtful. You will avoid having to spend money on a Mickey Mouse poncho if it rains.

• Before buying a rail ticket to visit Paris, check what sort of ticket would be best for you – you may be better off buying an inclusive day pass, which allows you as much travel as you like within a 24-hour period, at little more than the normal return rail fare to central Paris. Also have a word with the tourist office in Festival Disney about museum passes, free maps and so on.

• You need not worry if you leave your toothbrush behind; any Disney hotel shop can provide a replacement – but at a price that may surprise you. Take supplies with you of any films, medicines and so on that you may need. Disney hotels, while very comfortable, do not provide quantities of free bathgel and so forth. What you get is soap and shampoo.

• Above all, keep your children away from video games arcades. All the machines eat F5 and F10 pieces at a fearsome rate.

SPECIAL EVENTS

The Euro Disneyland band welcomes visitors

SPECIAL EVENTS

Besides the big parades that take place daily, or whenever the Park is open late, special holidays are marked by extra-spectacular extravaganzas. New Year, for example, witnesses even more fireworks than usual and parties in all the hotels. Special parades are held periodically throughout the year. Needless to say, Christmas is celebrated with carols and a tree. Other events are planned at shorter notice during the year.

If you are thinking of combining a visit to Euro Disney Resort with other major events, you will find Paris an ideal centre most of the time (apart from during August, when many Parisians leave the city for their holidays). In Paris fashion shows start in January. They are followed by the Paris Fair in April; the biennial Paris Air Show and Paris Festival in May; Tennis Championships in June, and special events to mark Bastille Day on 14 July. There are also the final stages of the Tour de France bicycle race to enjoy. During the autumn there is always a vast range of arts events, concerts, exhibitions and the like. The **French Tourist Office** at 127 avenue des Champs-Elysées, 75008 Paris produces a free leaflet called *Saison de Paris*, listing major exhibitions and events (tel: 47 23 61 72). If any of these coincide with your stay, book non-Euro Disney Resort accommoadation well in advance, to avoid disappointment.

Several other places within easy reach of Euro Disney Resort have special events, too. In Meaux, for example, there is a summer festival with *son et lumière* in the grounds of the Bishop's Palace. Reims, too, has its calendar, especially the viticultural one when champagne grapes are harvested. At Fontainebleau surprised visitors may discover a party of *belle époque* Parisians in splendid costumes strolling through the gardens, while Vaux-le-Vicomte offers tours by candlelight on some Saturday nights. The **tourist office** at **Festival Disney** can provide details of these events.

SPORT

Plenty of additional leisure facilities have been built at Euro Disney Resort to cater for the hours of relaxation when guests are not theme-parking and thrill-riding. These facilities are available *only* to guests staying on-site (that is, in appropriate Disney accommodation). If you like an active holiday, the best place to stay within the Resort is at **Camp Davy Crockett**. If you are staying at the campground you can play tennis, volleyball, basketball, football, *pétanque*, ride ponies (if you are small enough), bicycles (if you are not), jog round the running track, or swim in one of the Resort's loveliest pools. If you prefer to be a spectator, try out the **Sports Bar** at **Festival Disney**, where numerous TV sets show an endless round of sports programmes. Non-stop sports channels are available on Euro Disney Resort's hotel television network, too. All the hotels, and Festival Disney, have games rooms with a variety of video simulator games and other activities. Children's playgrounds are available at several of the hotels, and at the campground. The stockaded Fort Apache and Indian wig-wams are fun at **Hotel Cheyenne**.

Boating

Small motorboats called 'Toobies' – which look like large tyres, and take one adult, or a child accompanied by an adult – are available for hire at **Festival Disney**. More excitingly landscaped are the water-courses of Frontierland, the **Rivers of the Far West**, which run around that interesting piece of Arizona called **Big Thunder Mountain**. Euro Disneyland guests can traverse these waters in various craft: **Indian Canoes** (DIY paddling), **River Rogue Keelboats**, or two Mississippi-style **Paddlewheel Riverboats**. These rides, of course, are free once you are inside the Park, but they are popular and you may have a long wait for them on days when the Park is crowded. (Refer also to **What to See** on page 43– 48.)

Guests can paddle Indian canoes on the waters of Frontierland

SPORT

Croquet

Available at **Newport Bay Club** (for Euro Disney Resort hotel guests only).

Cycle Hire

At **Camp Davy Crockett** bicycles are available for hire by guests staying at the campground only.

Golf

The campground is conveniently close to the golf course, and it is open to the public. Golf Euro Disney is a championship course designed to host top tournaments, but less ambitious golfers of all abilities are welcome to test their skills. Lakes, hills, waterfalls, rocks and the most Disneyish bunkers have been magically bulldozed from flat arable fields, creating a series of varied landscapes which will eventually be sheltered by lush vegetation. Each of the three nine-hole sections of the course is rated Par 36, with lengths ranging from 6,781 yards (6,221m) for the championship course to 5,513 yards (5,058m) for the junior course. All facilities are provided: electric golf carts, a driving range, golf-bag storage and a putting green (in the shape of Mickey Mouse's head). The 19th hole has been provided, of course, at the circular **Clubhouse Grill**, whose windows overlook the putting green. Inside are showers, lockers, a bar and a restaurant, and conference space. Coaching, a repair and hire service, and a shop selling golfing equipment are also on-site. Green fees include the golf cart; group and package rates, and less expensive 'twilight' green fees, are also available. The course is open every day from 08.00hrs till sunset.

Health Clubs

The four more up-market hotels (**Disneyland Hotel**, **Hotel New York**, **Newport Bay Club** and **Sequoia Lodge**) have health clubs with gyms, saunas, solariums, massage, steam rooms, jacuzzis, and so on. Hotel guests can use them for F50 a day. A charge is also payable for the solarium and massage.

Ice-skating

That colourful ornamental pond outside **Hotel New York** freezes over during the winter months and members of the public can use it from 14.30hrs to 22.00hrs. It costs F50 for two hours (F40 if you bring your own skates); F30 for children under 12.

Jogging

There are two jogging trails, one around **Lake Buena Vista**, and one winding through the forest in **Camp Davy Crockett**. They are for use by Resort hotel and campground guests only.

Swimming Pools

If you are staying in Disney accommodation, one thing you should definitely bring is swimwear. The four most expensive hotels, plus **Camp Davy Crockett**, have heated pools. They are large and imaginatively designed, perhaps the most interesting being the one at the campground and the pool at

Sequoia Lodge, with its rocky waterfalls and woodland scenery. Euro Disney Resort guests should only use the facilities available where they are staying.

Tennis
There are four hard outdoor courts at Euro Disney Resort: two at **Camp Davy Crockett**, and two at **Hotel New York** (the ones at Hotel New York are floodlit at night). The New York courts are twice as expensive (F100 per hour) as the campground ones. They are all for use by Resort hotel guests only. Racquets and balls can be hired on site, but do remember to pack some suitable clothes and shoes if you fancy a game.

Ice-skating is popular in winter

Other Alternatives
If you are staying off-site (i.e. not in Disney accommodation), or fancy a whole day of sports activities, you can visit an outdoor leisure centre at **Jablines-Annet**, which can be reached from the N3 (exit at Claye Souilly). Visitors have access to lake swimming (sand beach), riding, tennis, archery, mini-golf, sailing, windsurfing and so on. A single modest entrance charge admits you to the centre; activities are extra. Groups can stay overnight; there is also a camp site. Tel: 60 26 04 31 for information, or ask at the tourist office in Festival Disney.

Directory

This section (with the biscuit-coloured band) contains day-to-day information, including travel, money matters and reservations.

Contents

Arriving

By Air

Most international scheduled flights, including British Airways, Air France, Aer Lingus, SAS and Finnair, land at Roissy–Charles de Gaulle airport, about 15 miles (24km) northeast of Paris (tel: 48 62 22 80). The other option is Orly, just over 10 miles (17km) south of Paris (tel: 49 75 15 15). Both airports are served by shuttle buses (*navettes*) which depart for Euro Disney Resort about every half or three-quarters of an hour (more frequently at weekends). Journey times vary slightly according to traffic density and the number of passengers

The Queen of Hearts' Castle

picked up. Buses cost the same from either airport (the fare is F65 single; children under two travel free). Passengers are taken to each of the Euro Disney hotels in turn, or dropped at the bus station, very near the entrance of the Park. If you are staying at Camp Davy Crockett, you can pick up another (free) shuttle bus from the station to the campground.

By Rail

The Parisian suburban railway (RER) now extends as far as Euro Disney Resort. The station is Marne-la-Vallée–Chessy, about two minutes' walk from the turnstile entrances of the theme park. Journey time is about 40 minutes from central Paris (Châtelet–les–Halles Metro link), but you need to be careful which train you take. It is a branched line (take Line A4, not Line A2 for Boissy–St-Leger), and not all the trains continue as far as Marne-la-Vallée. Check the platform indicators before you board, and make sure the correct light is showing. The single fare is F31 (1992 price). Trains run until about 00.00hrs.

By Car

Euro Disney Resort lies about 20 miles (32km) due east of Paris, off exit 14 of the A4 Nancy–Metz motorway (the route to Strasbourg) in the sprawling area of Marne-la-Vallée, *département* Seine-et-Marne. If you approach from another direction, to avoid the capital, you will probably use

Marne-la-Vallée–Chessy Station

the link system known as the Francilienne (A104 and N104), which traces a semi-orbital route around the east and south of Paris, linking motorways A1 (*Autoroute du Nord*, bound for the Channel ports, UK and the Low Countries), A4 (*Autoroute de l'Est*, leading to Germany, Austria and Luxembourg), A6 (*Autoroute du Soleil*, heading south for the Riviera, Italy and Switzerland), and A10 (*L'Aquitaine*, which goes via Bordeaux towards Spain and Portugal). Some of the new or upgraded roads around Euro Disney Resort are quite confusing, and traffic moves at high speeds. If in doubt, follow signs to Marne-la-Vallée (Val d'Europe) until you see *Parc Euro Disneyland* on signposts. French motorways are toll roads, so you will need some loose change handy. They are free in the Paris area, however (there is no charge on the section of the A4 between Paris and Euro Disney Resort). Leave the motorway at exit 14 and follow signs for the Park. If you are staying at a Disney hotel you can use the hotel car park; if not, park in the main lot (F30 per day for a car; F20 motorbike; F50 caravan or campervan – 1992 prices). The car park is huge (12,000 vehicles), so note carefully where you leave your car. Each sector is named after a Disney character. Moving walkways speed up the journey from the car park to the main entrance. Cars cannot be left overnight in the car park. If you have engine trouble, or forget where you left it, ask cast members for help.

'Point Photo' signs appear throughout the Park

Cameras, Films and Photography

Films, batteries and a developing service are available in any hotel shop and at several shops in the Park. The specialist photographic equipment store is **Town Square Photography** in Main Street, where you can buy or rent cameras and video cameras, and have film developed the same day. Look for the 'Point Photo' signs. You are not allowed to take flash photographs, or to use video cameras within attractions.

Car Hire

Europcar is the official Euro Disney Resort car-hire company, with a rental office on the forecourt of the Esso petrol station by the **Hotel Santa Fe**. Guests staying at the Resort receive concessionary rates, which are pretty competitive. If you are based at the Resort and just want a car to tour the area for a few days, this is by far the most convenient way to do it. Take the Europcar minibus from the hotel to the rental office. If you are staying off-site, check out competing rates at various airport offices. You can also book cars through Euro Disney's **Central Reservations Office** (see page 121).

Disabled Travellers

Ask for the *Guest Special Services Guide* at the main entrance, City Hall or any information booth. This gives full details of facilities for disabled visitors. The resort is designed to be as user-friendly as possible for all guests, but handicapped visitors will need someone in their party to lift them out of their wheelchairs and on to rides. Special vehicles can be provided to help guests reach the Park from the hotels or campground, and all hotels have rooms designed for the disabled. Parking spaces near the entrance are also available.

Wheelchairs can be rented from **Town Square Terrace** near the main entrance (F30 per day, plus F20 refundable deposit in 1992). Access to attractions, shops and restaurants is outlined in the *Guide*. Priority is given to the disabled for places to see parades and shows. Ask any cast member for advice. All WC blocks, shops and restaurants are accessible by wheelchair, and some shops have special

Moving sidewalks help take guests from Guest Parking to the Park entrance gates

First Aid and Medical

A first-aid centre with fully trained nursing staff is located next to **Plaza Gardens Restaurant** on Central Plaza, at the end of Main Street. Simple medical supplies can be found in all the hotels. If there is a serious problem, ask your hotel receptionist or the tourist office for advice. There is a pharmacy in **Coupvray**, a medical centre in **Esbly**, and a hospital in **Lagny**. Foreign visitors are advised to take out adequate medical insurance, even if they are EC residents. On a package holiday the tour operator will organise this if you are travelling independently you will have to arrange it yourself.

Guided Tours

These can be booked from ticket booths inside the main entrance. They last about 2 hours. Special VIP tours for private groups can be made, by arrangement.

Language

The two official languages in the Park are French and English. Visual clues are used wherever possible, but written signs, where they are needed, may be in either or both languages. You will learn some interesting new vocabulary. The shows requiring dialogue mix and match the two languages (with varying success). Most cast members speak the two official languages (not always fluently), and possibly others, the most usual being German, Spanish or Italian. There will always be someone who can speak these languages in Disney accommodation.

dressing-rooms. If you need assistance, enquire at **City Hall** or at **First Aid**, near Plaza Gardens Restaurant.
Most attractions are accessible by wheelchair If you have a weak back or neck, avoid the joltier rides such as **Big Thunder Mountain**, **Autopia**, **Star Tours** and the **Mad Hatter's Tea Cups**. Special aids are available for sight-impaired guests.

DIRECTORY

Lost People and Lost Property

Stray children are taken to the **Lost Children Office** near Plaza Gardens Restaurant on Central Plaza, where they are looked after until their guardians turn up. Enquire for them here, at any information booth, at **Guest Relations**, or at **City Hall**. Lost or found property should be notified to **City Hall** in Town Square, where you can also leave a message for separated companions (tel: 64 74 30 00). If you lose anything in your hotel, contact **Housekeeping**. Safe deposit boxes are provided at all reception areas.

Media – Radio, TV, Newspapers

All bedrooms in Euro Disney Resort hotels are equipped with cable colour television, currently receiving 12 international channels, including a news station and non-stop sport, plus five Disney channels, which relay closed-circuit information and Disney films. There are several radio stations, mostly featuring music. A wide variety of foreign newspapers and magazines is available in hotel shops and at the RER station.

Money Matters

Exchange facilities can be found at the **Main Entrance**, and in the two information booths in **Adventureland** and **Fantasyland**. You can also change money in **Festival Disney**, and (if you are a resident) at any accommodation reception desk. The rates given are standard throughout the Resort.

They are on the low side, but service is pleasant and efficient, and no commission is charged. You may get a slightly better commission-free rate in central Paris if you happen to be there, but it is not worth a special journey. Do not forget to take along your passport if you want to change traveller's cheques. Cash dispensers are available in the two arcades in **Main Street, U.S.A.**, and at the **Festival Disney Post Office**. All shops and hotels, most restaurants and the campground will accept major credit cards (American Express, Visa, Access); personal or traveller's cheques drawn in FF (with valid ID), Eurocheques, or even banknotes (French, of course). Euro Disney Resort hotel guests may charge items to their hotel accounts using a special card which they receive as they check in.

Opening Times

Euro Disneyland Park can be visited 365 days a year. Officially, the theme park opens at 09.00hrs most days (10.00hrs from November to mid-April), but often it is open earlier. Euro Disney Resort guests will find little notes in their bedrooms saying 'Just for you, the Park opens earlier'. Actually, anyone can get in if they bother to turn up. During peak seasons, you can usually get inside the gates at least half an hour before the official opening time, though not all attractions may be up and running. Weekdays are generally less busy than weekends, and **Tuesday** is an especially quiet day. On

Mondays many shops and other businesses are closed in France, so families often go out together then. Schools take a half-day on Wednesdays, and French children use this as a good chance to visit. Closing times change according to season, holiday periods, weather conditions and demand. Although the turnstiles may allow no more visitors in if the Park becomes too crowded, guests staying in Euro Disney Resort accommodation always have entry. Always check what time the Park closes as you enter. At peak times in high summer, it often stays open until midnight. Off-season the Park may close as early as 18.00hrs. (For full information about opening times, tel: 64 74 30 00.)

Some shops and restaurants in Festival Disney stay open all day; others open in the evening and keep going until well after midnight. Hurricanes shuts at 03.00hrs at the latest, but most other night spots close at 01.00hrs. The post office stays open until 23.00hrs, but exact times vary according to season. Most hotel restaurants serve dinner until 23.00hrs; bars may stay open later. (But not all bars open at lunchtime.) The best hotel venue for an all-day light snack is the Parkside Diner in Hotel New York.

The golf course is open from 08.00hrs until sunset, and the Clubhouse Grill stays open until one hour after sunset.

The main entrance to Euro Disneyland Park

Pets

The only animals allowed within
the Resort to compete with
Mickey and his friends are
guide dogs. Near the car park
is the **Animal Care Center**,
where trained staff will care for
Fido for a charge of F45 per
day, including food and
exercise (F65 extra overnight –
1992 prices). Pets are only
accepted at the Animal Care
Center if owners can produce
relevant certificates of health, or
proof of vaccination.

*Save time by getting
to know where things are*

Police

Euro Disney Resort makes its
own security arrangements,
very discreetly but very
efficiently. Security staff can be
summoned instantly to any
trouble spot, and will be about
five deep at any point in the
Park within just a few minutes.
Outside the Park, phone 17 if
there has been an accident or
you need the police; phone 18

for the fire brigade. Take sensible precautions with your belongings, as in any crowded place. Remember to lock your car, and do not leave belongings where they are visible.

Post Office

This can be found at **Festival Disney** and is usually open from 10.00hrs till 23.00hrs, seven days a week. You will not find it open on public holidays, though. Stamps can be bought at many shops, including **The Storybook Store** in Town Square, inside the Park. Postboxes can be found throughout the Park, and in the hotels and campground. All Euro Disney hotels offer fax services.

Reservations

To reserve accommodation or to hire cars at Euro Disney Resort, write to Euro Disney SCA, Central Reservations, BP 105, F-77777 Marne-la-Vallée, CEDEX 4, France. The office is open from 09.00 to 20.00hrs (French local time), or 08.00 to 19.00hrs (UK time), seven days a week; fax: 49 30 71 00 or 49 30 71 70. In the UK, tel: (071) 753 2900 (London office); from Ireland, tel: 49 41 49 10.

Senior Citizens

Groups of 25 senior citizens (over 55s) or more qualify for a 20 per cent reduction in Park entrance fees (this offer may not be valid during peak periods). Cast members are happy to help anyone with special needs. It may be worth getting a *Carte Vermeil*, valid for all women over 60 and all men over 65, which entitles the bearer to

reductions of up to 50 per cent in Paris museums, on public transport and in places of entertainment. The card costs F65 (1992 price). Take your passport to the *Abonnement* office of any main railway station, or the SNCF office on the ground floor of the main tourist office in the Champs Elysées. The card lasts a year. If you do not have one, wave your passport when you have to pay and you may still get a discount.

Telephones

Both coin-operated and card phones are available in the Park, in Festival Disney and in Resort accommodation. France Télécom phone cards are on sale at the post office, in shops, and at the golf course. Telephone charges are the same in all hotels and in the campground. They include a mark-up over normal France Télécom rates, depending upon what time of day you call.

Signs use pictures where possible

DIRECTORY

Tipping

Not necessary in Euro Disney Resort as a rule, though you may feel inclined to leave something in a table-service restaurant. There is no need to tip hotel staff for simply doing their job; for out-of-the-ordinary help, as you please. Outside the Park, check whether service is included (*tout compris*) before you pay the bill. It is customary to leave small change in a saucer at a bar or café. Porters, cinema usherettes, tour guides and, of course, Paris's laconic cabbies, all expect tips, as elsewhere in the world.

Toilets

There are lots of these, discreetly placed around the Resort. They are regularly cleaned and serviced and mostly exemplary, though some are a little cramped. Moreover, they are free. In this department, at least, the French could learn a thing or two from the Disney folk. What you will find outside the Resort – even at that modern miracle airport, Charles de Gaulle – is mostly best forgotten.

Tourist Office

Seine-et-Marne and Ile-de-France tourist office is situated in **Festival Disney**, and is a very good source of information and leaflets on local sights, hotels and restaurants. There is also a video and laser presentation. It is well worth a visit (tel: 60 43 33 33). See also **Excursions from Euro Disney Resort**, on pages 66–75.

Many modes of transportation are available in Main Street

LANGUAGE

Basic Vocabulary
yes oui
no non
please s'il vous plaît
thank you merci
hello/good morning bonjour
good evening bonsoir
goodbye au revoir
excuse me excusez moi
I am sorry pardon
later plus tard
now maintenant
small petit
today aujourd'hui
yesterday hier
tomorrow demain
week une semaine
when? quand?
why? pourquoi?
with avec

without sans
prohibited interdit
closed fermé
open ouvert
shop le magasin
stamps les timbres
bank/exchange la banque/le
  bureau de change
money argent
traveller's cheques chèques
  de voyage

Useful Phrases
do you speak English? parlez-
  vous anglais?
at what time? à quelle heure?
I do not understand je ne
  comprends pas
I would like je voudrais
this one ceci
that one celà
how much is it? c'est combien?

Directions and Getting
Around
here ici
there là
near près

before avant
in front of devant
behind derrière
opposite en face de
right à droite
left à gauche
straight on tout droite
street la rue
car parking le parking
petrol l'essence
underground station la station
  du métro
railway station la gare
ticket office le guichet
ticket le billet
ten metro tickets un carnet
a single ticket un aller simple
please direct me to pour aller à
the road for la route pour
traffic lights les feux
my car has broken down ma
  voiture est en panne

Numbers
one un (e)
two deux
three trois
four quatre

Shopping for souvenirs is part of the entertainment at Euro Disney Resort

five cinq
six six
seven sept
eight huit
nine neuf
ten dix
first premier (-ière)
second deuxième (seconde)

Days of the Week
Monday lundi
Tuesday mardi
Wednesday mercredi
Thursday jeudi
Friday vendredi
Saturday samedi
Sunday dimanche

Months of the Year
January janvier
February février
March mars
April avril

May mai
June juin
July juillet
August août
September septembre
October octobre
November novembre
December décembre
Christmas Noël
Easter Pâcques
festivals/holidays fêtes/jours fériés

Eating and Drinking
to eat manger
to drink boire
coffee le café
tea le thé
black/white noir/au lait
fresh orange juice une orange pressée
hot chocolate chocolat chaud
milk lait
mineral water l'eau minérale
a beer une bière
wine – white/red le vin – blanc/rouge
wine list la carte des vins

cheapest fixed-price menu menu conseillé
fixed-price menu prix fixe
self service libre service (le self)
waitress/waiter mademoiselle/monsieur
where are the toilets? où sont les toilettes?
all included service compris
menu la carte
first course hors d'œuvre/entrée
second course (main course) plat principal
cheese fromage
dessert les desserts
snack casse-croûte
may I have the bill? l'addition, s'il vous plaît?

INDEX

ACKNOWLEDGEMENTS

Maps and plans included in this publication are based on the Michelin Guide
"Euro Disney" © Michelin 1992.
The Automobile Association also wishes to thank the following photographers
and libraries for their assistance in the preparation of this book:
ANTHONY SOUTER was commissioned by the **AA Photo Library** to take all
the photographs for this book except those listed below:
AA PHOTO LIBRARY 66 Mercier Champagne (**Tony Oliver**), 70/1
Fontainebleau Palace (**David Noble**), 73 Moret-sur-Loing (**Barrie Smith**)
SPECTRUM COLOUR LIBRARY 74/5 Rheims Cathedral
© **THE WALT DISNEY COMPANY** Cover **Le Château de la Belle au Bois
Dormant**, 8/9 **aerial view over attractions**, 11 **Walt Disney**, 15 **aerial view
over attractions**, 28 **Festival Disney**, 44 **Big Thunder Mountain Railroad**, 97
Euro Disney Resort, 100 **Buffalo Bill's Wild West Show**, 111 **Ice-skating**